Marked Moments

Marked Moments

Lattice Boykin Mckoy

Order this book online at www.trafford.com
or email orders@trafford.com

Most Trafford titles are also available at major online book retailers.

Printed in the United States of America.

ISBN: 978-1-4269-9700-6 (sc)
ISBN: 978-1-4269-9702-0 (hc)
ISBN: 978-1-4269-9701-3 (e)

Library of Congress Control Number: 2011961399

Trafford rev. 08/15/2012

 www.trafford.com

North America & international
toll-free: 1 888 232 4444 (USA & Canada)
phone: 250 383 6864 ♦ fax: 812 355 4082

Acknowledgements

Mary Spearman Brown
High School Classmate
Magnolia, North Carolina

Olivia B. Jones
Honored Friend
Upper Marlboro, Maryland

Dorothy Boykin Johnson
Devoted Cousin
Elizabethtown, North Carolina

Delores Mckoy
Special Niece
Elizabethtown, North Carolina

Jackie Smith
Friend And Attorney
Jacksonville, North Carolina

Ingrid West Pendelton
Special Friend
San Antonia Texas

Anne Lee Matthews
Special Church Friend
Clinton, North Carolina

Marie Faircloth
Director Of The Senior Citizens
Garland, North Carolina

Loving thoughts and warm feelings are not only marked in my memory in this book for the individuals that I have chosen to write about, but for all individuals through-out the United States and other parts of the world who have played a role in making the world a better place to live.

Dedication

To
My
Husband

The late Romay Mckoy

What I want the reader to get from my book of poetry:

I want the reader to feel as President John F Kennedy felt about poetry. When he made this statement.

When power leads man toward arrogance, poetry reminds him of his limitations. When power narrows the area of man's concern, poetry reminds him of the richness and diversity of his existence. When power corrupts, poetry cleanses.

John F. Kennedy
October 26, 1963

Other Works by the Author

Moments of Pride, Passion, Prejudiced, & Sprituality
By Pentland Press Inc., 3132 Bar Oak circle
Raleigh, North Carolina 27612, USA
Available From Author
1-910-532-4673

Speak of Love
Xlibris Corporation
1-888-795-4274
www.Xlibris.com

Mr. Morris Deese

How marvelous
The strategy you use
To assist those who are,
Strangled and bullied
Even killed
While trying to live.

Thank you for standing up
To the animal in man
Tor the downed and dismal
Making them a priority
As they live on the edge
Of the land.

How wonderful
Such splendor
You must feel the pulse of God . . .
In such a quest.

Such passion
Looking out for the wronged
The cast aside and forgotten
What courage and compassion
To face these angry battles.

Mrs. Betty Ford

First Lady
Who received the biggest
Compliment of them all
A husband, President of The USA
Who claimed he was proud
To be her husband!

But, I know why
She was like a strong sharp goad
That ran without any special
Boundaries or limitations
Yet blossomed, and addressed
Issues, that humanity frequently
Try to obscure or second guess.

She was like a sword
That carried a forest
Of good will
And even in times of harvest
She told all the trees
And animals to stand still.

She knew who she was
And loved herself
Without pretentiousness
And never attempted
To be some one else.

If you didn't like her
For always being herself
That was alright
Because that was her gift
To those who didn't
Like themselves.
Brave, bold and bound
By the true soul of her being
Never asked for more
Than she would give
Learned the secret of life
That giving is receiving.

Perhaps, this is why
President Ford referred
To himself as Betty's husband
What a big ego for both.

Sam Cooke

Considered The Father of Soul
A popular and influential
American Gospel, R&B,
Soul, Pop singer, Song Writer
And Entrepreneur.

He is a legendary super star
With "A silky voice, and dashing
Smile."
His musical style, was said to be
Often imitated, but never equaled.

He became a household name
As he pursued artistic freedom
For himself and others
And seemed to enjoy his music
As he performed.

He loved gospel music,
Perhaps as much
As rhythm and blues
Because all of his music
Has a spiritual element
Of pride,presence and posterity.

His music seemed more
Than relating to mere man,
And seemed to capture
Other cultures, worlds
And times.

The artistry of his music
Seem to be a true gift from God
On loan to the earth,
Not of this earth, something
Outside of this earth
Beyond time . . .
That is called out
In the listener.

I feel that all of his blues
Have taken something
From the Gospel School
Which is like a thread
Tied around a cord
Or some precious soul
Speaking with the Lord.

Thinking about the father
Of Soul
With "that silky voice"
Will never grow old
If your fans have a choice.

There choice was to dedicate
An organization to preserve
Cooke's legacy
To meet annually
With family, friends,
And all who loved
His music.

TD Jakes

Make no mistake
This is a man awake
To the mastery of God.

Willing to praise Him
Every where
On the land, water,
And air.

Watch him
Listen to him
And you will know
All there is to know
About the Living God.

Catch a ride
On his mammoth
Spiritual wing
For he is swimming
In a sweet flowing stream,
Waving, begging and pleading
For you to jump in,
To take a swim with him
To the sweet elixirs of heaven.

What an amazing spiritual voice
Breathing the fires of God
In a life saving echo, wondering
How many souls can he save.

Eddie Murphy

A Stand-Up Comedian
Writer, Film and Television actor.,
And impressionist and singer.

He is a very popular comedian
Began stand-up comedy
As a teenager
And at age fifteen
He was doing impersonations
Of Al Green.

He was always on the rise
Named most popular boy
In his graduating class,
They could sense his success . . . .

Became a very skillful
Impersonator,
Almost an innate trait.
He claims:
"My mother said,
I never talked in my own
Voice."
What a great choice . . . .

Because when he personates
Bill Crosby,about his use
Of foul language,
He is so masterful
He manifests . . .
Not only the essence,
Of comedy
But he is truly magical,

And even more comical,
And foul in his response to Bill.

He is a talent
Who is highly imaginative
With a fast moving mind
Which will not stay any place
For a long time.

He has too many things to do
And so many ways
Of approaching them
To arrive at that
Eddie Murphy Effect.

Bill Crosby

A great humorist
Born with a laugh in his mouth
And when he learned to talk
He would spit a laugh out.

He could find a laugh
In any mouth
As he spoke with people
North, East, West and South.

Used his comedy
To go in and out of places
And at times, situations
As he walked through
Barriers of race
And had everyone
Laughing with him.

Communicates a relaxing energy
Giving birth to laughter
With the stories he conjures up
And that sentry of thought stuff . . .
Stops at every opportunity
To witness laughter
While playing the buffoon.

Learned early
To create with humor
The kind of atmosphere
Where he could teach people
How to laugh at themselves
And love it.

President Truman

I remember
He seemed most human
Sort of like an every-day man
Someone you see
And talk with every day.

But as president
He had some rather
Tough choices to make
And he made them
Without a whim.

When he took command
He had a plan
To stand, not sit
And take the high road
If he had to carry a stick.

He had control
Over the sea, land and air
After which,he had nothing
To declare
But war
And he did.

Called for desegration
Of the armed forces
And a civil rights committee
Dropped the bomb on Japan
And brought World war 1 1
To an end.

I know because
I was a cadet nurse
Trained to go to the war land
But President Truman
Had another plan
More fitting for the land
And he was a president
Who would take a stand.

The cadets were not needed
Over there
One of his last commands
Before he finalized his plan
To go home to Bess
Sit down in peaceful rest
And refer to himself
As, "Mr. Citizen."

Mrs. Bill Clinton, Secretary Of State

From Goldwater Girl
To First Lady Of Arkansas
To First Lady Of The United States
To Senator Of New York
Ran For President Of The United States
Became Secretary Of The United States.

She is smart
History will reveal this
And the whole world
Will feel her presence.

In the position
Of Secretary of State
Her wit, wisdom
And diplomacy
In working with others
Is most vital.

Too, she is most
Enterprising and savvy,
Never to be led
Down a blind alley.

Her mind can be
As hard as a stone,
But will melt down
If fed by the most
Cherished spoon.

She is a most judicious
Thinker
Alludes to no time,
For foolishness.
Listens to her heart . . .
And no one else.

This is a lady who reminds me,
Of what Steve Harvey said:
"Acts like a woman,
But thinks like a man."

She is fearless,
And advocates a philosophy . . .
Of, "We.", Not,"I."
Fully cognizant of the fact,
That together we stand,
Divided we fall.

She has placed a high priority
On a desire that all people
Hunger for,
Stated very specifically
In her first speech:

"Channel the currents
Of change, to a world
In which more people
In more places,
Can live up to their
God given potential."

Seek the fulfillment
Of this determination
History will acknowledge
You,
And the world will
Remember you,
Your time and your gift.

To President Elect Obama (2008)

Keep your hammer ready
Break through mountains
Of hate and ignorance
Never mind the resistance
For the change
That Martin Luther King
Spoke of
Is about to happen.

Time cannot wait any longer
For someone to be willing
To know something
Say something
To believe something
And to do something
Worth dying for.

History is calling
For an individual
That realizes
He is standing before
The gates of Heaven and Hell
And is willing to make a choice.

Make a choice, Dear one
Time will no longer allow us
To bruise and tarnish the truth
History is ready to promote
A freedom unknown to us.

And if you feel the hope
And freedom
For every man, woman and child
Articulated so elegantly
In your voice
The whole world is smiling.

Some of us never thought
We would live to see this day
For this is no act or Greek drama
You are going to the White House . . .
Appointed by God in His own time.

Mike Tyson

Notorious, "No"
Never found the world
A place to go
Or an open door
To feel his kind of truth
Or love.

Learned to find love,
Truth and his worth
By fighting in the streets
To survive
As a child.
Where he could,
Rather than be pushed aside.

He fought to live
And lived because he fought
Where winnings
Began in the street
Where he never
Met defeat.

He greeted the boxer's ring
With an iron jaw,
A copper swing
And profile of pain
With a killers instinct
That had to win.

Did you know you
Were a great fighter
Man of muscle
They knew . . .
Men whose names
Are written on your skin
We watch the tattoos
When you bend.

In the ring, you didn't see
A human thing, only pain
At intervals, you were back
On the streets again
Grinning that half grin
Where you could taste the win
And the good feeling,
It brought to your mouth.

That was your triumph
Like early street fighting
Anything to knock
Your opponent out.

Man with muscle of blood,
Great strength and reflex
Never indicating
Where he would hit next
Struck wickedly.
And unrepentantly.

Dedicated To Mr. Reagan

Renaissance man
With a grip of steel
Holds the gavel in his hand
With bridle and bits we feel,
The power of your command.

Renaissance man
Is there a secret sage
To guide a haughty clan
Of tough command in old age.

Renaissance man
What price must we pay
To wash our hands
In the holy water of today . . .

Renaissance man
Shall we pray
Or wait to understand
While our souls are swept away.

Renaissance man
Will there be better days
Is there a secret plan
In which we might appraise
The mystery of your command.

Simon Cowell

Lover of learning
Most discerning
Loves to see himself
In other people's yearning
Likes to make people hate
Forcing a certain truth . . .
In grilled debate,

To learn who is who
For no one really knows
And he knows that
No one has ever answered
All of his questions . . .

And all the while
He seems wickedly stubborn
Finds himself a wife
But becomes no one's husband.

Lives the life
Musing, thinking, being,
Himself
Without worrying about
What others think.

Letting the ID
Do the Ego's work
While the Ego, minds
The house of the Superego.

He looks out at man's
Castle of desire
And quietly chisels
Until he finds the welcome
Of a shaped claim
Of documented artistry.

Thurgood Marshall

You met the world
With great promise
And respect.
But was made to feel abject.

But you seemed
To know your own genius
And begged to serve
With a passion so great
You remained undisturbed.

When institutions
Of higher learning
Turned you away
For not being White
Something, you couldn't,
Do anything about.

But you changed the signs
On the doors, that wouldn't
Let you in
Broke the minds of people
That didn't want to bend.

You came
You conquered
Taught that segregation
Wasn't right
And taught the law of things
Day and night.

Now your name
Is inscribed on a building
The building of law
At a university
That rejected you.

A true lover of your work.
Giving yourself to help people
Comprehend the law . . .
Perhaps, helped the nation more
By achieving a place
On the Supreme Court
Thank you Mr. Justice . . . .

"Barbbra" Streisand

Changed her name
From Barbara,
Is one of the world's
Greatest entertainers
She sings, acts, records
Writes and produces
Her artistry is phenomenal.

Broke the barriers
For the female
In film production
Founded The Striesand
Foundation with several
Other actors.
And The First Artist
Production Company.

Striesand's artistry is manifested,
In songs, acting, and producing
Within the entertainment
World,
And the expansion of women . . .
No women, in the history
Of the entertainment world
Can be compared,
As exercising such passion
And energy.

She scripted,produced,
Directed and starred
In Yentl.
Won two academy awards
And nearly a grammy

For every performance.

Considered the best
In practically all of her performances
And was labeled "An all-around
Female entertainer."

She seemed determined
To do her best, and she is,
The "Best."
It seemed that her aims are
Higher than the sky
Positioning themselves
On a heavenly landscape
Near by.

Listen to her sing,
"Evergreen" and,
"The Way We Were"
Then you will feel the
Great spirit and passion
Of her artistry.

Her great artistry
Is magnified in her philanthropy
And it is hardy
Her response . . .
Is, she wants to give back.
And how she has given.

Elizabeth Taylor

A goddess of love
No one has matched
The caliber of her beauty
And the allure of men.

A beauty that stood high
Above the ugliness
Of life
In her powerful approach
To the abandoned, rejected
Misfits and misunderstood.

Born with this beauty
And love
Owned herself
In spirit and soul
And never seemed
To worry about the talks
And tales of life.

Remained steady and diligent
In her intent, to give herself
To those whom society
Had turned their back on.

With all her beauty
She had a remarkable
Aesthetic sense, and loved
Beautiful things, not always visible
To the eyes of others.

This gift could be seen
In her beautiful eyes,
Eyes that always seemed new
And surprised.

She was a most bejeweled
Woman, physically and spiritually
Very whole and complete
No half—way individual
All or nothing at all
Lived a wonderful witty
And worthy life.

The arts and sciences
Will record,
That she had it all,
Beauty, soul and the
Spirit of love.

James Taylor

An American Guitarist
Song Writer
Plays Blues and Folk Music
Who learned to play the cello
In North Carolina,
But switched to the guitar.
And wrote his first song
When he was fourteen
Years of age.

Taylor formed a band
Known as "The Flying
Machine"
Seemed to have an innate . . .
Grasp for music
And sense of Melody.

It was noted that his
Mother heard him
Singing,"What a Beautiful
Morning"
When he was only
Seven years of age.

Taylor has had many
Hospitalizations for
Feelings that made him
Feel down,and unenergetic
To perform, and display
His musical genius.

These illnesses seem
To awake these sleeping
Musical giants,
And he would come back
With another musical hit

Manifesting,
That he is a Great Song Writer.

Pardon me,
I believe,his artistry
Is his healing,
Not only for himself
But for the world
Of his audience.

His illnesses, perhaps,
Permits him to say in song
What he can't say in
Ordinary conversations,

And serves as his vehicle
Giving him the muscle
To dig deep down
In to his soul of music,

To share with people
That joy and sorrow
That is not easy
To handle
In ordinary rhetoric.
And build on that propensity
To express a lot of love
In his musical artistry
As well as a lot of trust and
Faith.

I get these feelings
When I listen to:
"You Got A Friend,"
And, "Bridge over Troubled
Waters."

Oprah Winfrey

Oprah Winfrey
Is she done?
Not yet
Think of her long
Fruitful run.

In those twenty-five
Years of fun
Touched by God . . .
It had to be
For God didn't make but one
In all his great pottery
From the great state
Of Mississipi.

Her favors seem
To excel all others
A big soul and a gigantic reach
Tried to make us sisters and brothers . . .
More than a caress, more than a speech
Something so rare, something so deep
Sort of like giving the lane man feet.

She doesn't know the wealth of her success
How she made everyone see some of her
In themselves,which is rarely identified
And often hidden from themselves.

Got people talking openly
About things that had been hidden
In the dark closets of their lives
Trying to function through fears
Of what people would say.
Perhaps, that's why so many of us
Were so inspired to travel with her
On her long fruitful ride
Because she taught us how
To be proud of ourselves
No matter what our secrets are
And that we will learn
That we are as good and bad
As the other fellow
When we take a look in our closet
Or dream his dreams . . . .

Rev. Jessie Jackson

Where are you
Where is the passion
That chose you
For the action
To help people.

You used to be
So intense
Seemed like helping
People was all
You wanted to do,
I am anxious to know
What happened
To you.

I followed you
To neighboring countries
The Vice Presidency
Candidacy,and
Your Cival Rights prodigy.

Watched most of the
Long presences, and studied
The doctrines
Of your work
Saw you crying,movingly . . .
On the television screen
As The First Black President
Walked through.

Please put that, "Push,"
Back in your hand
The one you founded,
The one I came to understand
The one that made you
Best friend to man.

I keep your photo
On a special table
Because I think
Your grasp is stable
In your message from God.

Smokey Robinson

Mr. Robinson is an American
R&B Singer, Song writer,
Record Producer
And former Record Executive.

He is a legendary Motown Artist
Smokey had contemplated college
When he met Berry Gordy
A song writer,
Berry became the founder
Of The Motown Label
And appointed Smokey
As his Vice President.

He also became part of a group
Known as the miracles
He not only created hits for
His group,
But a wide variety of other groups.

His hit songs, also earned him
The title, America's Poet Laureate
Of Love
The Beatles were influenced
By his style and grasp
John and George admired
His work, and paid tribute to him.

The Beatles loved his work
In 1976 George Harrison
Paid tribute to Smokey
In the song, "Pure Smokey."

Bob Dylan said,
"Robinson is America's
Greatest living poet
ABC recorded a tribute
Called, "When Smokey Sings."

His popularity continues
To grow
As does his honors, awards
And accolades
He was mentor on the popular
Television show, "The American
Idol
And continues to receive
Honorary Doctorate degrees.

His genius can be perceived
Not only in the quantity
But in the elaborate girth
And quality as well.

Mr. DickChaney, Former Vice President Of The USA

You have always had my complete
Attention
From the time you were appointed
Vice President Of The United States
I was surprised . . .
With your long-standing health
Problem,
But presumed
This is an individual
With A Very high esteem
And chutzpah
Or he would refuse the position.

But you served in the position
Where your resignation
Was ever ready
For your service to end
If your health didn't win.

And you served us
To the end of your term
Resonating many bends
And turns
But never failing
To articulate your concerns.

Which always seemed to be
Unique and different
At times, an opposite view
From those of the President
But my thoughts and opinions,
Wasn't worth discussing
The event.

But now since you are
Out of the office of the
Vice President
I wonder why
You have taken on
The voice of discord.

For example, It was stated
That you said, "The Secretary
Of State, would be more capable
As President
Than the President.

If so, why words of discord
So unworthy of a heart
That has worked so hard
To keep you on the job.

You speak about
The father of the country
Pitting father and daughter
Against each other
Claiming that she could
Do the job better.

Who can gain
From such a statement
No one.
And the country may lose
Some confidence
From the creator of discord.

We all
Have a right
To speak out
But the country's business
Is not a game of girl scout.

It is no good for the
American family
To pit the daughter
Or father against
Daughter
What do you hope . . .
To achieve
For the American family
And the country as a whole?

Maya Angelou

Queen of the home
Where the sweet words flow
Into one's heart
And out of the door
To be host of the wise . . . .

A poet,one of a kind
Combed many worlds
With a fine tooth comb
Knows what its like . . .
To feel alone
And be right at home.

The likes of her
Will not be seen again
Making words her chariot
Dancing on the clouds . . .
Knows the magic of life
And is proud.

A woman of letters
Espouses a rhetoric
That knows no fear.

Learned early,the beauty
Of the written word
And the certain death
To not know, or ignore it.

Now we all can smile
With Maya Angelou
And be amazed
By her incredible style
Of writing.
In her Queenly approach.

Rest with the gods
And she belongs to time . . .
Find her
Get to know her
From afar
Listen when she speaks
And you will know
Where you are.

Nancy Reagan

First Lady
President Reagan's wife
Whose greatest accomplishments
Were his love, and contentment.

She was always there for him
And he knew this . . .
There was no storm or pain
That she would not resist
Or insist to be near him.

He was her God
And she his angel
As he read his love letters
To her.

She was never too far
To listen to him
Because she lived
Inside of him
As he gave his love
So eagerly and freely.

Sharing his love letters
With the world
Proving that love
Has no shame.
As they felt the acclaim,
Of loving and being loved.

And to realize
That love conquers all things
She his queen
And he her king.
Not only for this life
But for always.

He was at the podium
She was always on the stage
And even when he had to leave her
She held her place at his grave
With the sweet spray of flowers
That stay, with the inscription,
"With love always."

Senator Edward Kennedy

How congress and the whole nation
Must miss you, and your passion
For getting things done
Even if you had to cross the isle
No one took your joy and pride.

Imagine your being there now
When most of your congressional
Fellowmen,can't find a suitable chair
To bring food that is edible to the table
Or to share
Tabling every thing
While the neophytes complain . . .
Creating hostile atmospheres
Seeing how many people
Will lend them their ears.

If only you were here
You would find a chair
And a table, with food for thought
To share with the opposite party

So that we would not be in the street
Begging for bread.

I can hear you saying
Party or no party
It is the people who count
And if we fail them
We will have committed
The impardonable sin
And no one will win.

Toni Morrison

Born on a high song
Sings all day long
Never had to feel or yield
Or think she didn't fit
Or had no talent to achieve . . . .

She was born with a golden brain
Never felt the prejudice or pain
Or that fast growing weed
That made other children bleed.

From a most disciplined brain
Writes as she sings
She always has command
With a very deft and special brand.

Gives solace and strength
Always stretching the length
Makes the weak feel strong
Writes about the wronged . . . .

Takes solitary trips like the eagle
To better know her people
Will she fly pass the Pulitzer . . .
With all that special inner luster.

Vice President Gore

You ran for President
But God had another intent
More becoming ?
More geared to your personality
More akin to your artistry.

Your attention to detail
Yet, seemingly detachment to man
For the immediate sentiment,
May be difficult
To understand
That your destiny . . .
Is more tied up with the land
And the universe.

Inexplicable to ordinary man
You looked pass man to rehearse
A place, a time, where you could plan
To be are not to be president.

To consent to follow another design
Within the hidden flaws of time
That seem to have no rhythm or rhyme
Pointed to a certain area of unrest
Which seemed to be your quest.

Malcolm X

Took the test
Of telling Black people
They could be more than they were
Even more than they could imagine
Themselves to be.

What a frightening
And dangerous precept
In a world that is not free.

Risky
To have these idea
Especially, revealed to one
Who has lived on chance
And promises
Always living on a skirmish path.

But he walked this chancy road
Boldly, and spoke a fermenting
Language
Met no thinker like himself
Because he told people
What to do
He did not ask.

He was a man
We didn't understand
Perhaps ahead of his time
With big ideas and strong mind
Without a strategy for the time
To deal with those who doubted him
Or to find growth and development
In an erosive and barren land.

President Roosevelt

Known by his initials as F. D. R.
Came into the Presidency
In the middle of The Great Depression
And pulled us out.

Congress approved his New Deal
For economic and social recovery
And when he took the steering wheel
He did not waver or yield to the hard times
He drove through them
With an ingenious mind.

He was the potter
A most mentally energetic president
We were the clay, ready to be modeled . . .
As he rationed the way
To make us content.

He held the gavel high
It was always steady in his hand
He taught us how to do or die
With the New Deal Plan.

Visiting Peer Mediation Presenter

He was there
Like an African Prince
Claiming he needed no accolades
Only many prayers of strength
For the streets he had paved.

He was there
A nd planted a learning tree
In the center of the hallway
To prove that we were free
To learn, to laugh, to stay.

He was there
To teach us how to build a house
When we reached the highest limb
Teach others to learn to espouse
To help those on a lower limb.

He was there
In a gifted, yet passionate stance
To identify, and precisely declare
That learning was a romance
Where each person had a chance
To Begin to look for love.

Tuskegee Airmen

Forerunners of the civil rights movers
Destroyed the breaking hearts
And the myth
That you couldn't or wouldn't
Dare to fight for your rights.

But you pulled your wings
Out of the sky
To box with the clouds
Making your hearts proud
Of physiques that were limitless
And matchless in range
With a passion for eating pain . . . .

Ushered in:
New pursuits
New thoughts
New routes
For all of us . . .
With chutzpah
That stayed on top of the game.

With teeth made of iron
Cut deep into the gates of steel
And copper plates
Took a dare with time
Leaving no time for debate
And flew away
With pieces of love and devotion.

Practiced at Moton Field
Ordered by President F. D. R.
Named The Negro Pursuit Quadron
Created by God . . .
And gladness held their hands.

Josephine Baker

A giver and a taker
A great entertainer
Dancer and singer
Who danced on the table
To prove to New Yorkers
That she could provide
Food for thought.

Her talent spoke for her
But not in the USA
Because it was not ready
For her assortment
Of boldness of style.

A talent so raw and rare
Was not accepted here
Nor the way she chose
To express her self
In her dance of life.

So she brazenly
And disarmingly
Took France
Like a mighty storm
Bottled all her charm
And like a praying-mantis
Kissed her on the arm.

Clothed in rhythm and rhyme
She beat the system
To sing, dance and dine
To become their girl.

Betty White

What a delight
More than a golden girl
Like a coveted pearl
From the salt land
Of the sea.

A real osyster
So richly endowed
So veritable and vibrant
So proud
That time moved
Out of her way
Giving her space,
To refine and design
While she can enjoy it.

What a legend
A woman
We can call,
"Forever,"
That delights us all the time
When if ever we will find
A soul of such divine.

Frank Sinatra

Chairman of the board
With a voice
That carried a sword
Of sweet melody.

It was knighted in gold
Sweet harmony on every edge
Made the young and old
Ready their ears and pledge,

To listen to him,up or down
Medicine for the bruised soul
You can hear him in every town
Strong, soothing and bold.

He carried his song
Where ever he wanted it to go
He was king of his throng
And when he sang
He told you so.

Kate middleton

To Kate Middleton
I put myself in your place
A commoner
Who fell in love
With a royal subject
And looked yonder
So private, yet public.

In all the wonder of this love
All the wit and wisdom to inspire
Would I be able to hold my head up high . . .
While the subjects quietly inquire,

Does she really love him
Or just seeking a high place
On the chart,
Or a commoner
Riding on a whim
Being very witty
Yet very smart.

No, she is a rarity
Part of a divine plan
Perhaps an altered destiny
Transformed by both
God and man.

Michael Jackson

Michael Jackson
Prince of music
And wonder of the world
With a never ending passion
For his music
That he gave to us.

His music
The only life
He had
He gave it away.

He gave away
His most precious jewels
In a passion so raw and rare
In a desire that called
For all of himself
And he answered
To that most urgent call.

His music
Was his food
Not just for thought
But his gift to the world!

We the world
Crushed the jewels
Like swine,
We cast them underfoot
Never realizing
That he was trying.

To tell us how much
He loved us.
We made him prey
To our dark choices
Never realizing our losses.

Now we weep
Even in our sleep
When we remember
His dancing and singing thriller
Wearing the white glove
Believe he was trying
To tell us, in all of his shyness
It was all about love.

Prince Williams

Walk proudly down the isle
With your darling bride
While people stand on the side . . .
Of this Godly event
And sigh in wonderment.

Just be charming
Realize that God is not asleep . . .
He is merely yawning
But he has allowed us
To enjoy this epiphany,

To ready yourself
To wed, and rule a nation
With God's good wishes . . . .

The world will never
Ask more of you
Than the Mother Queen
To believe in your ability to lead
But always be considerate . . .
And generous
Like your mother.

Thank You

Thanks to all of you who came
To whom our sorrows share
For sharing our stinging pain
Or said a little prayer
And even those who couldn't be here.

Kin-folks how you surrounded us
In every act and word spoken
Almost prompting us to think
That the circle was unbroken.

Church and friends
How you saluted us
With kind words and songs of joy
While the pastor spoke of God's plan
And ideas we all can employ.

To all the great health teams
UNC, SRMC and Quinn Hospice Center
On your philosophy of care we leaned
And your loving care remember.

We thank Summerville and Boykin Mortuary
For their creativity during this sorrowful event
And God who allowed us to rejoice and be merry
For a life that found a high degree of contentment.

Written following the death of my husband,
Romay Mckoy, November 4, 2009.

Michelle Obama

First Lady
Has the charm of a queen
And the familiarity
Of the woman
We see next door.

Walks with balance
Between the good and bad . . .
And comprehends both.

She is the queen
That sits on the throne,
Of pride, charm and style
Simple, yet special.

No lows and no highs
She teaches us
To reach for the sky
So that we will have the chance
To remain above the ground,

And stop sitting on the edge of time
To imagine
What it is like
To be full-fledged individuals.

Ode to The Policemen

You are in a position
Not far from God's,
And must handle
A variety of Godly roles
To up-hold the divine plane
And while on this earth
You trod,
You must be a friend
To man.

Prepared to give your life
To save mine
If that's what it takes
What a sacred price . . .
To be so divine.

You live the oath
Every day of your life
While some of us . . .
Laugh and boast
That your job
Is no sacrifice.

But you do make sacrifices,
At times, just watching
The store,
While many of us . . .
Ride out to the shore.

Too many of us
Leave others unprotected
And rarely close the doors
To hate, anger, and death.

The policemen
Hear our cries for help
They come in the middle
Of the night,
When everyone else
Is hidden and out of sight.

The policemen
Is not just any man
Who walks casually by
He is trained to do all he can
Even when we fail to comply . . . .

The policeman
Is a humanitarian
And a good Samaritan too
Helps people
Who are left helpless
And left by others
To die
On the wayside of life.

The policeman
Will stick closer
Than sisters and brothers
Or lovers.

The policeman
Is a stand –up man
Or woman,
Each day, standing up
For you and me.

Some times he or she,
Has to protect us from each other
Other times from ourselves
Without being able
To fully protect him or herself.

Love and respect the policemen
Think what the world
Would be like without them,
And know that the gift
Of appreciation
Is all they need.

Stop and salute them
On your busy day
Don't wait until their
Is an emergency
To call them and say,
"Knowing you are there.
I feel happy and safe."

Letter To President-Elect Obama

The spirit of Martin is in the air
J. F. k's legacy, still inquires,
"Why not?"
Robert, his brother claimed . . .
There was enough opulence
For all.

Imagine President Reagan's
Optimism
Being put on the spot
And LBJ looking back
At the civil rights pack.

Carter's surprise at your
Discipline
Is something to declare
As Clinton,
With his intellectual curiosity
Said, "I'll be there."

Colin Powell, a military man
Crossed the isle, saying.
"We can."
Malcoln X with a brain
Of gold
Didn't Know how to think
For the whole.

F. D. R. claimed
You have nothing
To fear, but fear itself
But you are saying . . .
Rather refreshingly,
"I am using my fear,
To claim myself."

Now you have made
A big pancake of fear
And invited all of us
To come near.

We will, possibly
Be invited to the
White House
For breakfast
If we can conjure up
The muscle of syrup,
Since you have melted . . .
The butter down
All we have to do
Is come down
Off our stirrups
And learn to walk
On solid ground.

Toney Bennet

When you sing
You make the people
Of all the world
Feel like kings and queens.

You mesmerize us
In a harmony of love
Its sheer magic . . .
The way you embrace
And tenderly caress
A single word.

So effortlessly
You soothe
And mold, seemingly
Saving one from
A less loving thought . . .
In the tenderness
With which you sing.

You share so boldly
An inner melody
Of a precious soul
Which speaks
Of an internal joy
With self and life.

Sings so soothingly
Allowing the melody
To run down your mind
Like fresh blood
Running in your veins.

Solid, steady and soul-feeling
As the pulse, of joy
And satisfaction is emitted
You seem to share
An inner bond
With humanity
Which makes the audience . . .
Want to see the music sheet.

There is a kind of magic
That you exude
Perhaps, without being
Aware of it.

When he walks in
The audience seem
To make more room
Than he needs
For, in the splendor
Of his artistry
He makes space for
Everyone to feel that
He is singing just for them.

God must have
An ever expanding hand
To gift you with such command
And abundance of time.

Paul Newman

Came from a well—to—do
Family
His father was a business
Man
But Paul left the store
And went into acting
After special training
At some of the finest
Institutions.

What an actor!
Favored by the gods
Handsome
With a lingering
Sexual attraction,
And eyes as blue
As the sky
On a fair day.

Paul was a very popular
Actor
Who became a screen
Legend.
Winning all the prestigious
Awards
Including The Life Time
Achievement Award.

He seemed to have lived
A great life
One that he personally
Enjoyed.

A super star
A passionate race car driver
And business savvy
A restaurant called the
"Dressing room,"
Created his own salad dressing
Developed a summer camp
For children
Had a happy home
And was loved by the world.

Bob Hope

You are no joke
But you are really funny
And that's the way
You planned to be,
A master mind
Of comedy.

You are a reality
You love to make
People laugh
Even when it makes
You look like a fool.

I have followed you
Over fifty years,
Half of your life
Felt many cheers
And humorous advice.

I have watched you
Make the world laugh
Until they almost cried
As you walked a happy path.

You visited our troops
In practically every land
Not just once
You had a continuous plan
To share your joy
Of living, with them.

You are a treasure
To the world, especially
To The USA,
With that fine sense of humor
And acting ability too,
With a wit and wonder
That made all your
Wishes come true,

And big promises
That you made as a child
Wedged into words of comedy
That when you found out,
You, "you couldn't be King
You left Britian."

But you are king
Of comedy,
Who gives commands
That is always a joy
To hear.

What higher king
Can you be
When you are skilled
In saying things
That make people happy.

Andy Williams

A charming singer
Made Moon River
Every one's song.

And when he sings it
We can see
Moon river running
Smoothly on and on.

What a crooning talent
Nicknamed,
"The Emperor Of Easy"
Giving his voice
A golden touch
No rushing or hurrying
The rhythm too much.

His music is so sweet
And calming
Cataloging one's longing
And unrest
Sort of a subtle warning
That harmony is best.

In his moon river theater
Though I have never
Been there
I know he is the creator
Of a new world
In every heart that hear
Him sing songs
Like moon river
And the calming element
That is always there.

Aretha Franklin

Queen of soul
And gospel's friend
Singing gospel way back then
Revolutionized the gospel song
Then went on to soul's home
Where her artistry has led her
To make more room,
For the world
Of music.

To all the world
She is a legend
Sharing her gift
With the man next door
And every work shift
At the ball game
The church
She is the same . . .

Shared the momentous
Moment of the first
Black President:
President Barack Obama
How she sang!
At this celebrated event.

There are no parallels
As her voice took wings
To rest in the history
Books of time.

But, I heard the mention
Of a most striking hat,
She wore

That seemed to make
Her artistry, even more
Comprehensible
To the ordinary man.

And I am proud
Because it is good
Even masterful
When man can see
And appreciate the
Genius in the woman or man
That lives next door.

Mr. Arnold Schwarzenegger

Model, Hollywood action hero,
And star
Body builder, generous philanthropist
And was governor of a seemingly
Ungovernable state,
Yes, all of this makes one question,
Was he destined to be great?

The answer is a question, still
Whose destiny has not been fulfilled
A stranger in town, "No."
He has only a few more miles to go
Before we will know him.

A stranger in town
Would not know the scope
Of what love and honor is
And be fully cognizant
Of the dreams they sought
And realize they were
Out of harmony
With these favorites.

Did the Id crush the days
Of your youth and longings
As the Super-Ego bowed
In anguish prayer
To speak no more . . .
Of the high places
You sought.

Now, the one mighty Ego
Frail, fatigue, and fraught
With desire
Had no energy . . .

Nor soul and spirit to guide you
Through the once safe waters
That flowed so sweetly
To the sea,

Did you seek the stale, stagnated
And still flow
With its loss of freshness and fluidity
Which had become smelly
And odoriferous.

Allowing one to regress
To the behavior of the terrible two's
Where the child is prompted
To touch and fiddle
With every gadget in the home
At times putting them in his or her mouth
Seldom foreseeing the danger or harm.

All was pleasure
And pleasure can't wait
For the child in us . . .
You didn't mean to cause alarm
Remember, in retrospect
You are favored by the gods
Full of wonder and charm . . .
For making your position
A little easier
By having invited you
Into their home . . .

The dreams you sought
And the walk you walked
Think!
Did you gain as much
As you lost
And as a model, body builder

Hollywood star
Philanthropist
And governor of California

Were you considered great?
Are your destiny . . .
Being fulfilled
Perhaps,
But it has been altered
In all its richness
By the dark shadows
Of unspoken pain
That may never be alleviated
And a harmony . . .
That may never be restored.

B. B. King

The legendary
Blues king
A long reign
To explain
His love relationship
With the blues.

In his music
He makes sorrow
Laugh and sing
When he sings
The blues.

When he sings
He gives the blues wings
You can see the sunshine
In the rain.

When he sings
The Thrill Is Gone
You feel the joy of the pain
And the thrill all over again
As it takes wings
Like a cool and refreshing wind.

With that expectant look
Of passion and desire
And you feel like you
Want to cry . . .
His blues soothe
And let the sadness
Rise to the sky.

He gives the blues
A home of delight
And when he sings
Sad and melancholy feelings
Discovers a healing
That gives them strength
To rise from near ground level
And feel the blessing of heaven.

Yes, he makes the blues
Feel like Sunday gospel
And the elation of the old hymn
You feel free, and forgiving
For the thrill that held you fugitive
Is gone
As the king of blues
Sings on.

Barbara Jordon

Congress woman from Texas
Maker of history
Referred to as the
Voice of thunder
That rained down on
The halls of congress
With wit, wisdom
And wonder.

She walked
The bridges of courage
Often in fueled debate
Crossing many dark waters
And numerous fields of fate.

Long before the evening
Of her work was to end,
She waded on the shallow edges . . .
Of injustice, gender and race
And in her own magnetic words
Made her pledges-
Dried her wet, soaking body . . .
And cemented her place,

Among the giants of politics
Rose from the dark waters
Of time, and design
To the highest mountain
Of thought and pride
Where her words,
The voice of thunder
Still reside.

In her call for greatness
She left us some of that thunder
That we heard in her voice
Some of that wit, and wonder
To help us make the right choice.

Barbara Walters

Journalist and author
First American Lady to interview
Individuals from practically
All parts of the world,
What a connectedness . . .
How enviousness and arousing?

But I don't think its all about
Who you know, as much as
What you know.

You have something
That every woman wants
And that every man fears
"Smartness", that is so quiet,
So graceful, and silent,
Which, perhaps, cannot
Be heard or seen
By the average ear or eye.

You are like a breath
Of fresh air, on a hot humid day
When the forecast has called
For rain.
Or that sudden feeling
Of great vitality
When someone pushes
You in a swing.

You are unlike any
Other journalist
That I have known,

In the social and interviewing
Realm,
You seem to have an inborn

Propensity
To know how to climb
The social stairs
And when to hold
On to the banister
When coming down.

You convey to everyone
I am here for you, don't worry
Whatever it is,
I'll see you through.

You see so much
Without saying a word
Just setting in a room . . .
Your charisma feels so near
By just being there.

You are like a favorite
Corsage
With confidence to spare
Which doesn't seem
To be involved
But, it stays there
In that special place
Serving the purpose
It was designed to serve
That's how thorough you are.

When one review s
The talents of you

Life is like an open door
That you seem to enjoy,
Walking through.

Benny Goodman

Known as the King of Swing
"The Professor,""Patriarch
OF The Clarinet"
And Swings' Senior Stateman."

He was also called a jazz great
But his greatest contribution
To jazz,was to accept
And launch the careers
Of major names in jazz.

During the era of segregation
He helped to make racially
Mixed groups more acceptable
And jazz more respectable.

Jazz was not considered
Respectable music in 1938
But different groups loved
This new and strange sound.

Benny said,"If a guy is got it,
Let him give it.
I am selling music, not prejudice."
And continued to be The King
Of Swing.

Benny's father, sent him
To school at the age of ten
To learn how to play the clarinet . . .
And he played in his first pit band
At the age of eleven,

And became a member
Of The American Federation
Of music at the age of fourteen
In his meteoric rise.

He was the first White band leader
To challenge segregation
And hired African American Greats
Such men as Loniel Hampton
There-by encouraging . . .
The growth of jazz.

In 1938, The Benny Goodman band
Duke Ellington, And Count Basie
Made history, as the first jazz band
To play in New York's prestigious
Carnegie Hall.

This concert was dubbed:
As jazz's coming out party
To the world of respected
Musicians.

This was a triumph
For jazz, the Great Afro-Americans
Musicians and Benny
Mostly for Benny,
A stickler for perfection
And there is no perfection . . .
In jazz,
Its perfection perhaps,
Rests and resides in the soul
And sound of its creator,
And beholder.

Benny maintained his interest
In classical music,
But history will always record . . .
His gift to jazz.

Berry Gordy

An American record producer
Founder of Motown Record
Label
An idea man,
With almost clairvoyant
Eyes
Maker of legends.

Prince of ideas and thoughts
Knows when the water is hot
Can smell gifts of talent
Miles away.
Knows when talent meets
The stars
And whom the stars
Will shine on.

Knows what makes people
Laugh, dance,sing and pain
He looks inside the mind
Takes a seat . . .
Being no half-way person
Then stands tall,
And sweeps the mind clean
To know,

When to listen
When to talk
When to sit
And when to walk.

Maker of legends
What an empowerment

Savvy in his business quest
And has the chutzpah
To know how far he can go.

Being a man of all seasons
Can see a man's promise
In deep snow . . .
Takes a risk in the wintry
Weather
To get to know . . .
The promise of a kiss
In every endeavor.

He Knew that people
Could be educated
Through songs,
And how they touched
The human spirit
And entertain.

He knew what he was looking
For,
And understood
What he saw.

Look at him!
With that wise and calculating
Smile,
Which reveals:
I'll eat it, and relish it
If you got it."
I'll make you a musical Legend

Meet Stevie Wonder,
Diana Ross
And Michael Jackson
They are the life
And music of legends.

Berry is The American
Record Producer
Who found them.

Billy Holiday

A jazz singer for all times
"Could swing like,
Any great horn player."
And had the voice of an angel.

Touched all souls
Within reach
And some that were slightly asleep
That had ever heard her sing.

She had a golden voice
So sensitive and sweet
Seem to have been picked
By choice.

She sang so soothingly
Yet, inquiringly,
Enough to touch the heart
Of the lost soul.

But never seemed to speak
To her,
And through hard living
And sad songs
That seemed unforgiving
Of the wrongs
That visited her.

Yet, she gave us
Songs in a musical voice
Of rhythm and rhyme
In the gaffs of her time
That cannot be duplicated.

Or replicated.
She gave it all to us
Leaving her with none
But strife, to die . . .
Never to fully know
The luxury of her voice

Mohammed Ali

Changed his name
From Cassius Clay
Most appropriate, Sir
No clay feet for him
No flaw or weakness
Anywhere
That he did declare.

The man: A champion
One of the greatest
In the land
That he did declare
In a little litany
That he was, "The Greatest."

He always said, he was
The greatest
Because he believed
In himself
With a mind of iron
And rhetoric of fire
Who wouldn't be
Afraid of him.

Yes, he could fight
And he was handsome
In the ring
One could watch
The movement
Of his hands and feet
Without hearing him sing
And come to realize
This man was,
"The Greatest."
In the boxing ring.

Chris Rock

Named at birth
Christopher Julius Rock
He is a famous Stand-up
Comedian, an Impressionist,
Actor and movie star
Creator of "Everybody Hates Chris."

When I looked at his picture
On his biographical data
I saw something in his eyes
That startled me.
He had such a serious profile
Nothing like he looks now,
With a mouth full of laughter
His mouth was tightly closed
Probably, holding in the world
That only he could create.

In the first place,
His profile was more stern,
And serious looking
His eyes seem cast
On another world
With a distant look
Looking over and pass
All of us.

Firstly, I saw ambition
Courage and independence
With a hint of defiance.
And the message
I perceived Was:
"I can take what ever

You give me
Just hand it to me
And watch."

Mr Rock is still functioning
From our meager world of thought
And the world he spied . . .
Many years ago,
Has just begun to unravel
And he has begun to speak
To it.
With a clarity
Only he can wrestle with
Because he is the only one
That can seek his own destiny
And acknowledge it.

Claims The Hilarious
Eddie Murphy is his mentor
But his mouth is not half
As foul as Eddie's
His down and dirty words
Reminds me of a kid
Who is trying to shock
His mother
In to seeing his reality,
Or test the waters
Of acceptance and rejection
By his audience.

But, foul words are words
That were once fresh, and in great
Demand,

Before they were contaminated
And painted with ugly behavior
And unacceptable chances.

Frankly, I like some of it
Especially when framed
To depict, describe, explain
"Or tell it like it is"
That's real comedy to me.

You are a fabulous comedian
On the stage or off the stage
You know what is funny
And what is not funny.

Chosen as number five
In Comedy Central's 100
Greatest
Voted the Funniest Person
In America by Entertainment
Weekly
And welcomed the largest
World audience in London
And in 2003 received
A star on Hollywood
Walk of Fame.

"Mister Rock" you are a rock
And you are a wise nut,
Too,hard for me to crack
So,I have decided to sit
On the side, and chat.

Preferably,
In words of poetry
This is how I will attain
My, "Piece of The Rock."

Chuck Berry

One of Rock and Rolls
Great lyricists
And a guitarist that no one
Could follow.

He is a pioneer
Not only in his grasp of songs
But in bringing Whites and Blacks
Together.

He was one of the first
To know that he had the appeal
Of all people
Because he played
To all people.

He is a pioneer
In Rock And Roll
Seems like it blended
With his soul.

He played them all:
Jazz, Classic, Rock and Roll
Country too,
He could take his guitar
And make a musical brew
With a hop-scotch like
Movement,while playing
To connect with
His audience.

He is a great showman
Seems to have great fun
Just tinkling with his guitar

Making it often appear
Like a shotgun
And when you watch
His gestures as he moves
Across the stage
You begin to feel the fun
Of his early-play –days.

He influenced the might
Of rock and roll:
With the Great Beatles
The Rolling Stones
And numerous others.

Charles Edward Anderson
Known to us as Chuck Berry
Is considered,
The Father Of Rock And Roll
A great inspiration to us all.

He is honored in The Hall Of Fame
A clip of his Johnny B. Goode,
Was chosen to be played
In Voyager I Spacecraft.
Think of his legacy.

Condolessa Rice: Former Secretary Of State

Condolessa Rice
Secretary of state
What a price
A Black woman
Staged to page the nation
While it is still
Having growing pains.

The first,
In a position
Where no Black woman
Has ever stood.

Born and bred
In a boldness
Of biasness
To race and gender.

A position
Never intended for her
Though talented
In both the arts and sciences
As well as serious questions.

She walks
In grace and splendor
Wasting none of her beauty
On souls that do nothing
But squirm . . . .

She was put there
To flavor our souls
Like an old spice
Knowing when to speak
And when to not
A person of all seasons
And a gift to the world.

Count Basie

An American Pianist, Organist,
Composer and bandleader
Was the first leader
Of a Kansas City Style
Swing Band to rise to
National fame.
He was considered
A leader of one of history's
Most influential Big Bands.

His mother taught him
His first piano lessons
And as he played by ear.

He learned to improvise
And developed an unusual
Sense of rhythm,
That he always seemed
To Listen for throughout
His musical career.

Count required that all
Of his music "have feeling"
With superb arrangement,
Good taste, and "sterling"
Performance.

With his innovative talent
He used two saxophones
Players,
When most bands
Used only one.

His band was noted
For its rhythm section
Where the rhythm is high

In such tunes as:
One O'clock Jump"
And "Jumping At
The Woodside.

Basie favored blues,
"And show cased some of
The most notable blues singers
Of the era: Billy Holiday.
Big Joe Turner and
Joe Williams.

His music had a rhythm pulse
And was loved world-wide
By both the old and young . . .
Some favored the swing
And some favored the jazz.

But his greatest gift
To the members
Of his band
And to the world
Was his enthusiasm
His consideration
Of the musician's opinion
Relaxed manner
And fun-loving ways.

Because of these qualities
The band had the greatest resiliency
One of the most thriving
And one that is assured
A place in history.

Denzel Washington

A most handsome man
Been referred to as the
Sexiest man in town.
And America's favorite
Movie actor.

But, today,
As I looked through
Material that
I had collected
For my People's
Museum,
I ran across your photo
On the front of Ebony
Magazine,
March 1994.
"The Hottest Black Star
In Hollywood History."

But I saw more
Coming from deep
Inside of you,
A man of high choices
With dreams and wishes
To own himself.
But more importantly,
To thank God
For favoring him
With not only
His good looks
But for giving him
A good view of life
And seeing him through,
The complexities of life.

Called, "A man with connections,"
Possibly, one of your
Greatest assets
Even more vital than
Your good looks
Because your contacts
Help you to keep
In touch with self.

You have been described
As America's Favorite
Movie actor
I will allude
To this commentary,
Especially when I see you
In: "Glory," "Philadelphia,"
"Malcolm X,"
And, "Cry Freedom."

For Dr. Mcphail, At The Sampson Regional Medical Center, Clinton, NC

The Physican, Pregancy, Poetry And Me

He stood there
In the door way of his office
Handsome as and elm tree
Casting his eyes
Upon the middle of me,

In a gaze, momentarily
Like a kite caught in a tree
In thoughts that, seemingly,
Had nothing to do with me.

Then, he smiled and said,
Rather explicitly
Yet, somewhat teasingly,
"Are you pregnant?"

"No, not for the life of me,
Never been so vibrant or free
Where something good
Could grow inside of me,
That can cry and laugh
Be empowered to love
And be loved
No, it is some other growth
Out side of my scope.

Nothing but my poetry
Grows inside of me
My book of poetry
Is my pregnancy
Something that sets me free
And brings out the best in me."

What nice thoughts of him
I thought it was a malignancy . . .
Or something,
That he would have to do
Surgery on me.

Seeing me, thinking inside of me
He said, "No malignancy,
You are free
To plant that poetry tree
There is no need for surgery
Your book of poetry
Can very well be your pregnancy."

How magically!
All he could see
Was words growing inside of me
That was destined
For all my books
Of poetry.

Now, as I complete
This book of poetry
I feel his generosity
And what he said,
About pregnancy
Poetry and me.

Dr. Mehnet Oz

I love a good renaissance
For you make seeking help
Like a new romance
All is splendor and glory.

Like a first love
Everyone is falling in love
The sick find love in the square
Healing is in the air . . .
Like the image of a pretty woman
With a rose in her hair.

You put your hands
On the heart of hearts
Making an art of healing
Sounds like a love song . . .
Revealing how the heart loves
The renaissance doctor.

A true lover
Never turning his back
On the eyes of the soul
And the Hippocratic Oath.

Making blunderers
And would –be scoundrels
In their bubbly effervescence
Stand at the square
With their mouth open,

Quietly inquiring
Where did he come from
Out side of the womb
Or is the belly his home

So much room
For both the bride
And the groom.

Whether the belly or the womb
He is here
Never mind about
Where he came from
God holds the spoon
That he feeds us with.

Calling out caressively
Meeting all of man's needs
In the sweetness
And purity of his soul
In a romance of healing
Which we all clamor . . .
With our camera.

Is there something
We never observed
In the curriculum
Or never learned,
The art of pacifying
And the vision of peace . . .

Perhaps he sneaked
Pass us
While our heads were turned
Making us yearn to see
More medicine men
With such humanity.

Duke Ellington

Was a musical composer,
Conductor and band leader.
Who helped to originate jazz,
And became the greatest
Jazz composer of all time.

He began to play the piano
At age seven
And created his Jazz band
At seventeen years of age.

He was a man ahead of his time
In ideas, thought and philosophy
And quoted that man,
"Was a god in ruins
And that a problem
Was an opportunity
To do something."

This philosophy
Perhaps, influenced
And guided him
To reach his potential
Because, in actuality,
He never saw a problem
He saw opportunities
To advance himself.

With this attitude
He saw himself as a god
Not ruined by life
But, a great inspirator
Endowed with great creativity . . .
And created,"one of the most
Distinctive esemble sounds
In western music.

He was highly prolific
In his music
And took his music
To the Cotton Club
Who catered to "White Only"

But his music was so explosive
And un—colored,
His color didn't seem to matter
Too, he was a sophisticated man . . .
Who had learned the art
Of being eloquent,
In early training of the arts
In art school.

He was exquisite
Probably born that way
For, in his teens his friends
Called him Duke
Due to his elegant
And flashy style of dress.

But they didn't fully realize
What he was saying by his
Style of dress,
But he related the same message
In these three songs:

Mood Indigo, Sophisticated
Lady, and It Don't mean A Thing,
If You Don't Have The Swing.

He was a realist
And when times became hard
During the depression years
He went in his pocket
To keep his band going.

History will reveal
That he is a legend
And espoused,
One of the most distinctive
Sounds in western music.

His tributes are legion
And he is still receiving honors
16 honorary degrees
Medal of honor
From president L. B. J.
And president
Richard M. Nixion.
1986 a commerative
Stamp
And Sir Duke
Written by,
The Great Stevie Wonder
In honor of him.

He was a "Duke"
Grandeur in style
And lived it
Had No feelings of insecurity . . .
And possessed great mastery
In getting the magic
Miracle, and magnificence,
Of his work across.

Who else could have written
Sophisticated Lady
Only the man,
Who said that each problem
Was perceived as an opportunity
To do smething.

He was quite fruitful
And used the magic
And promise in his life
To inspire others.
With that open-book—smile . . .
And mouth held wide
Where laughter couldn't hide,
He used his masterful
Approach to life
And the quality of appreciation,
To help others
Who got bogged down
With what he called
The ruined man.
Who lost his ability
To live like a god.

Ella Fitzgerald

A great singer
And musical improviser,
Came from a very lowly . . .
Beginning
To become, "The First Lady of Song"
And was the most popular jazz
Singer,
For more than half a century.

In 1938 at the age if 21
She became famous
After singing, "A-Tisket A-tasket
A nursery rhyme.

All the great singers and musicians
Claimed she was the best
Because, she not only had
A very beautiful and sultry voice,
She could imitate any instrument
In the band.
She would often say:
"If you can't sing it,
You have to swing it."

She would master scat singing
Turning it into a form of art
Using her voice to take on
The role of another horn.
It was said that she stole
From the horns
But I would proffer
That the horns stole from her.

Ella said, "I sing like I feel."
And the audience loved her
And she liked being loved.

The fans made her feel
Better about herself
Than she had ever felt
Because she was totally
Accepted.

She claimed, that there was
One debt that she wanted
To pay,
That debt was to:
Marilyn Monroe
Who stood up for her
When she was not accepted
In a small club in Texas,
Marilyn came every night
For one week.
After this, Ella had no more
Problems, of a racial issue.

People, the world over
Loved to hear Ella sing
America, dubbed her:
As the, "First Lady of Song"
Kids in Italy called her
Mama jazz
Mel Torme, called her
The High Priestess.

Ira Gershwin, once remarked,
"I never knew how good
Our songs were
Until I heard Ella sing them"
Andy Williams claimed,
"She brings out the best
In everyone,
Making everyone work
That much harder
To keep up with her."

Chick Webb,the great musician
And band leader
From Baltimore, Maryland
Was her mentor.,
When he died he left
Her the band,
She not only sang
But imitated every instrument
In the orchestra.

I was in high school
When she sang,
"A –Tisket A-Tasket"
And thought,
When she opened
Her mouth
Diamonds fell out,
In that gripping
Energy and breath
Of love and happiness,
This is a voice
That I will never forget.

To All Firemen: Especially those that are, (living or dead), that participated in all of the recent tragedies: Katrina, 911,hurricanes, tornadoes and the onslaught of tsumani waves in neighboring countries

Ode To Firemen

We will always pay tribute
To you in songs of love
And prayer
In endless praise of you.

And the memory
Of your divine pledge
To a job, to do
Whatever is required
Of you.
In a job that is never
Through.

The rewards seem so subtle
In such a horrific plight
Fighting one of the elements . . .
Like the sea, and the graveyard
That is never satisfied
Or feel it has enough.

Oh the beautiful blessings
You must feel and prioritize
Knowing that fire is hell . . .
But you feel a greater prize.

The passion to help or save
Is so huge, it shades
All your doubt

As you run to the fire
Seemingly, without flinching.
Like a minister . . .
Of the Holy Word
Trying to save souls,
Walks in any catastrophe
Realizing there is no guarantee
That you will not be burned
Or die
Trying to save another's life.

We praise you
We honor you
And we adore you
For living out
Your God given potential
With a free and loving spirit.

As we mourn those of you
Who did not survive the plight
We feel indebted to you
But when we think
Of that liberating light
That guided you,
We happily come together
And express words
Of how we remember you
With Love.

In the bright light of hope
And life's sweet revery
May we always devote
A special time

To celebrate.

On these hallowed grounds
Where you earned the right
To live in eternity,

Sit down!
Where there are no more
Fires that harm
Or earthly alarm
In the light and fires
Of delight,
That illuminate
The warm fires of Jesus.

For those firemen
Who still serve us so fearlessly
Giving all that they have
With a bright and loving
Soul
Be proud
For you possess a genuine
And bright energy to help
Others
That many of us will never
Know or comprehend.

But, for the most part,
You are loved
Even if someone forget . . .
To tell you so,
Your gift of love
Will be recognized
By the name
On your front door.

President Carter

A southern man
Who believes in the power
Of the land to grow
Things
That are better
Than ourselves.

Seems to be
A christian
Always holding out
His hand
To help others
Be more healthier
Free of disease
Have a nice home
World wide . . . .

But these good
Old southern ways
Didn't seem to be
As magnificent
When played out
In the White House
As president.

Remains more powerful
As an ordinary citizen
Helping others
To be better
By having the opportunity
To live better.

But Mr. Carter
Is no ordinary man
He belongs
To another time
Another land
Not made by man.

And perhaps
As president learned
A better route
To be of service
To man
Something all men
Should learn early in life
To make life more
Precious.

General Petreus

Referred to as one
Of the Great Battle Captains
Of American History.

Taught soldiers how to think
As well as how to fight
A visionary . . .
Envisioned the future
Didn't like what he saw
And commanded change.

He is a master strategist
Lauded as a most honest
Individual
In all of his proposal, strategies
And commands.

He never called victory
Too soon,
Or when, or to whom
Always giving himself space . . .
To hear, see, and feel
And document the end.

He is a great innovator
And founder:
A think tank
Of designated
Thinkers
The Petreus Guys
And Petreus Doctrine,
Based on his fierce military
Knowledge, education
And global approach.

In wartime history
You are matched,
With Grant, Marshal
Pershing and Eisenhower.

General Petreus
With that, "forever,"
Forward look
America regards you
As a legend . . .
For the many battles
You undertook
Home and abroad.

President Dwight Eisenhower

Military man
From Abilene Kansas
Waited thirty years
To lead men into battle.

Served under Pershing
And MacArthur
West Point graduate
And proved to be
A great strategist.

Fought in foreign lands
But it was difficult
For him to use force
Or develop a plan
For that same type
Of freedom
In his home land.

As president
He met racism
Face to face,
The army was still
Segregated.

Being the president
He followed the Constitution
And sent some of his men
To help governor Faubus
Quell the mob.

He was sad, to learn
That there was no
Easy peace at home,

Order by force.
Being the president
Required him to lead
In the integration at home
Something
He was not required
To do as a general
In a foreign land.

But time would not
Wait
So he sent the federal troops
To escort the nine Afro American
Students into the Little Rock
School
Because governor Faubus
Had refused.

He claimed, This was
The saddest day of his life
But a great general,
Especially of his stature
Should be quick to realize
That peace does not
Come easy
And rarely without force.

But he did what he
Had to do
And the world can be
Proud of him.

J. K Rowling

Had a mind explosion
Of a masterful fantasy
Much more than
A vivid imagination
On her way home
One afternoon
Which astounded
The world.

Her mind rose up
In front of her
With a lot of ideas
And thoughts
From other worlds
About something that
Would excite and intrigue
Every boy and girl.

She had to jot it down
All the energy and inspiration
That she thought she had loss
Seemed to swell up in her throat
And give her a toss
To make the choice
To write
Harry Potter.

Yes, In her downed doors
And windows of her soul
A youthful and magnetic spirit
Sprung forth, and stayed
With her, until she had finished
The Harry Potter saga.

No relief or satisfaction came
Until it was finished
And the freedom of self restored
That's the gift of genius . . . .

J. K Rowling
Will never be the same
Neither in this life
Or the other
After writing Harry Potter
And those who read it . . .
Will possibly
Conceive and experience
New visions.

Jackie Robinson: The Great Ball player

How dark was the night?
When you came out
And put the ball
Where we could see it
From the back seat.

You tricked the night
Out ran it
And wouldn't quit
Until you reached the day,
Where there was enough light
For Black boys to play
Even at night
And learn to become . . .
More comfortable
In their plight.

With every accolade
You thought about us
And picked up
The dead wood
Without a fight,

To free the ball
You flew many skies
Making a lot of stars
Eager to touch the ball
That you held iin your hand.

Now we count it all joy
Prompting the angels to sing
When you out ran all the pain . . .
Without shedding a tear
Or losing one drop of blood
Turned hate into love.

Jacqueline Kennedy

First Lady
Beautiful
Beyond measure
In more ways than one.

Wore the pill-box hat
With queenly pride
Weaved a many . . .
Side walk chat,
That never died.

But the pill-box hat
Symbolized more than
This or that,
It displayed a hint of healing . . .
Amid the political dealing.

Very private
A model
Of good taste
And wore it
With elegance
That seemed to
Parallel Sainthood.

What a winsome one
A diamond
Well polished
With a glitter
That shone like
An evening star.

A beauty from a-far
She didn't have to say a word
To reveal her beauty
All she had to do
Was to walk down the isle
Into a room
And leave the door ajar.

Johnny Carson

King of the late night show
A title he rightfully deserved
No one seemed to possess
The skills, wit and humor
That Johnny seemed
To have been born with.

He was a great showman
And knew what the audience
Expected of him and his show
And he never disappointed
Them.

Johnny was like no one else
He found a comfortable home
In bringing out the best in others
And had great fun in doing so.

He seemed to be holding
A looking glass
Viewing every one
And every thing
So he could have
A clear view.

Better still
A quick snapshot
Or a flash
Of the inner abilities
Of people, was all he needed
To put on the show.

Thus, he selected
The most accomplished
But, there were large
Numbers of unknown talent
Whom he helped
To develop their artistry
Because he was gifted
In bringing out the best
In the entertainers
That he invited on his show.

He helped people
To get in touch with their art
And to learn how to enjoy
Sharing their talent with others
And while giving so much
The greatest gift
Was to themselves . . . .

He gave entertainers
A chance to play house
Like kids
And to grow up, get serious
Deal with life's adversities
More than any other individual
Of this century.

He was a legend
He knew how to entertain
And how to help entertainers
Give their best.

It were as if
He was wired to their soul
With identifiable pathways
To the rest of us
So we could fully
Enjoy their artistry
And talent.

His brilliance and talent
That he was probably
Born with,
Took him to places
In our hearts
That few people
Have dared to go.

Lady Bird Johnson

First Lady
Lady Bird,
Your legacy lives on
In the million of blooms
That find their home
By the highway side
Kissed by your smile . . . .

We are never lonely
In our long travels
When the flowers wave at us . . .
As they hold on to the magic
Of your beauty.

They will always be there
To remind the nation
That you planted them
Some, during the dark days
Of the Vietnam war
A time when there
Was no beauty and peace
To share

But you planted flowers
Where,
No one can block
Their stare
And their sweet
Breath of love.

Now long past then
We can visualize you
Standing in the middle of them
Throwing kisses now and then
As they begin to bend.

Lady Ga Ga

Rising up in the world
Like some torpedo
Electrifying
Like dynamite
Or maybe lighting,
Just as spontaneous
And uninhibited.

She appears on the stage
Of life
So very different
From any one we have
Ever known
Unprecedented
A world phenomenon
Acquainting us
With many worlds
Of entertainment and joy.

She seems so magical
And illuminating,
Far beyond the roots
Of time
Where everything
Is new or unborn.

To see someone so new
In their being and approach
To the world,
Is refreshing and invigorating-
Like pieces of the finest
Hors d' oeuvres
Made into a sizzling stew.

We all, can't wait to meet her
How our appetites are whetted
Especially, the youth crew . . .
As we all marvel at the wit,
Wonder and the individuality of her.

Lady Ga Ga
If you were "born" this way
The place you came from . . .
Must have packed your bag
With the rarest of creative thought,
Filled your heart with the gift
To understand the differentness
Of others
And a mind to not only
Take charge of self
But your thoughts as well.

Write the songs we love
Keep on dancing
Into our hearts
Act out our dreams
And fantasies
As the queen of differntia.
Who holds the
Principal concept,
I would rather be nothing,
If not myself.

In summary, I see her
As the Renaissance Woman
Who has touched the world
With her bold and brave
New approach to
The world of entertainment.

Lionel Richie

An American song writer
Musician, record producer
And actor.
Grew up on the campus
Of the Great Tuskegee
Institute.
Once a member
Of the musical group
The Commodores.

Richie went solo in 1982
Most of his songs
Seem to show a great
Appreciation for ladies
And are very romantic.

Listen to, Three Times A Lady
And Lady, the song he wrote
For Kenny Rogers,
Truly and Endless Love.

Hello, is my favorite
It has a warm neighborly
Yet universal touch
But most of his artistry . . .
Is popular world −wide.

His accolades and awards
Are numerous
Both in the USA and the Uk
The George and Ira Gershurn,
And The Lifetime Achievement

Award
Are perhaps, his most cherished.

He is a great song writer
And the world will agree
With me
As they listen to:
Hello, Truly, Three Times
A Lady, Dancing On The Ceiling,
All Night Long,
And Endless Love.

His gift is further portrayed
In the fact that he can create
A song for every mood or feeling
That a person can possibly endure
Bringing joy and healing . . .
That's for sure.

Louis Armstrong

Nicknamed Satchmo
Considered the Father of Jazz
Rose from a home
Where no child should have
To live,
To be hailed,
By kings and queens.

Had a "rough beginning."
Had no help in the beginning
Mother in the street
And father some where else.

In his teens he got in trouble
In the street
And was sent to a delinquency
School
Which seemed to be his first
Real home
And proved to be his best.

There he found love:
Music.
And learned to play
The cornet
And played so well
That he was asked to be
The band leader.

With this blessing,
That seemed to twist
The hands of fate
He not only survived,
He began to prize himself . . .

Switched from the cornet
To the trumpet
And with this new self-concept
Began to improvise
And made tunes of jazz.

Although, he had a band
That he played
All over the land
The trumpet took command
And spoke for him,
About playing the trumpet
Like no one else.

He was a great improviser
And inspired musicians
To improvise
Using their own unique style.
And as a renowned trumpet player . . .
Changed the course of jazz.

Satchmo was not only
A great trumpet player
He was a singer, soloist,
Comedian and band leader
Who improvised wordless
Style singing, known as "scat"

He guided the creative out put
Of such figures as, Duke Ellington,
E lla Fitzgerald and Dizzy Gillespie
He brought joy to the bandstand . . .
"As a trumpeter, singer and band leader
And has yet to be matched."

Even now, when I hear him play
The trumpet,
And Sing, "Hello Dolly"
And, "What a wonderful Day"
I am awestruck by his joyful
And sensuous delivery
He was a true virtuoso . . . .

Lucile Ball

Being funny was her call
She knew how to make you laugh
Even if she had to crawl.

She walked a funny path
And seemed to feel,
Her own comedy
Laughing so happily.

She was funny to the bone
Seemed to feel so at home
As her body seemed to say . . .
Have a happy day.

She was like a fluffy cloud
That no rain ever came through
She would smile
And laugh loud
For me and you.

She could take something sad
And make you feel glad
With the humor that she had
Even when she tried to look mad.

She must have been born
On a laughing machine
That made laughter scream . . .
A way into your heart.

No matter what ugliness
Came into her path
She would do something
That wold make you
Sit right down and laugh.

Marilyn Monroe

Movie star and actress
A classical beauty
Born that way
Still lives in a way . . .
For she was a lasting beauty
And had a beautiful soul.

She was real
But very few people
Saw her in her own skin
She was merely a fantasy . . .
Or a beautiful butterfly
With clipped wings.

But, "The First Lady of Song"
Ella Fittzgerald,
Claimed she owed her a pearl
For opening doors
That were closed
To let her in.

And said,"Marilyn was
Ahead of her time."
I am inclined,
To agree.

When I read her quotes
I could understand what she said
All she ever asked the world
Was to see herself as herself
That would have been
Sheer happiness.

But that is something
The world never addressed.

When she uttered,
"Hollywood is a place
Where they will pay you
A thousand dollars for
A kiss,
But only fifty-cents
For your soul."
They may have . . .
Bought a kiss
But she never
Sold her soul.

I think I know why
She was always
Late for her performances
By a quote she made,
It took something from her
That she was unwilling
To give away,
A chance to stay
A little longer
With Marilyn
And honesty . . . .
.

Taking something from herself
That she had reserved
For herself
Truthfulness . . . .

She only wanted
The,"Right to twinkle"
And twinkle she did
Always truthful to herself
To the very end,
But the world
Would not let her in.

September 8, 2009
Marine Dakota Meyer

In the battle of Ganjoal
Battled with the arms of war
To save his team
Nearly, and at times
Single handed
Took command
With his own plan
To live or die.

To save his team
At any cost
No other thought
Gained access to his mind
But to answer their call
For help.

His bravery revealed
The image of a man
Whose eyes held the
Look of both life
And death.
His nose a pointed
Sword,
His mouth shaped
In a tighten commitment
That would take the breath
Of any enemy force.
With his arms in an ever
Encompassment.

You are a hero
Accept it
Your team who
Gave their lives . . .

Would be proud
Of your valor
And smile on your favor.

No other living individual
Of our time
Has offered up his life
So freely.
Something that can't
Be replaced.

Most of the individuals
Of your honor, your pride
Love, valor and selflessness
Are dead.
But you were favored . . .
To live, to tell the story.
Think about what you have to do
No one can tell it better.

The president
Conferred upon you
The medal of honor
Because he knew
What you had been through.

And is going through
And that you did it for
Your country,
The standard bearer
For all of us.

You gave to all of us
Your self
Something few individuals
In the course of history
Have willingly done.

Be proud for the
Rest of your days
Continue to wear the bracelets . . .

With the names of your
Team members inscribed
On them.

Don't frown on your life
Say a little prayer,
Or dream a sweeter dream
And remember,
God gave you something
For you to smile about
And that you
Have to have His
Permission to die.

Mark Zuckerburg

Prince of wonder, thought and time
Where did you obtain such a mind
Having us talking, living and giving
All over the world.

What an idea
To scatter the word
Where people all over the world
Can chat with each other.

You had a desire
"To make the world more open,
By helping people connect and share,"
Taking us places where angels
Fear to stare.

Your hands have reached
Across the valleys and mountains
Of time
Where we all can achieve
A new birth
To live on a new earth
When we think of how many people
We can chat with in a day's time.

Run on young one
Catch the falling sun
Before the rain comes . . .
With that brazen energy of mind
Making us to live in a different time . . .
Because you wanted us
To be more open
Now the task is spoken.

Because of you
The world will never be the same
For that little vehicle that opens
Up the doors to share
Has never been tamed
And when the dye is cast
Can cause a lot of pain.

Yet just to hear a sweet voice,
At times is worth the cost
To have been there
For until your genius was shared . . .
To think of talking to people
All over the world
Was like a chance to speak
To someone in heaven or hell.

Now we are miniature gods
We can share what's important to us
Never have to meet each other face to face
In reality we can change what we say
For the tongue has never been tamed . . .
It can travel down any lane.

Yet, in many ways, I think Facebook
Is a good thing
Perhaps mixed
With a lot of glory and pain
While helping us to find
That part of self
That can only be noticed
In some one else . . . .

Oh! What an invention
Perhaps the invention of the century
Where people are born again . . .
Touching base with more of themselves.
Opening doors and windows world-wide
Closing barriers to race, culture and language.

Martin Luther King

That Seemingly Far Away Dream

Martin you did not die in vain
Though the dogs at times still bark
You took the fire out of the pain
And gave us a good start.

That, seemingly far away dream
Marking the highways of our time
Lights through the fog –a gleam,
Of loving thoughts that bind.

In this year of twenty and ten
We sit in the town's civic center
Where White Folks are our friends
Feeling great honor and adventure.

The Mayor, our first White speaker
Spoke proudly of your legacy
Urging each of us to be the keeper
And reap the dream's prophecy.

Martin, all the things you worked for
Is like a Greek drama to this generation . . .
And, as we experience a bit of joy
They too, show some appreciation.

Today, that seemingly far away dream
Where Black and White hold hands
Is occurring more often than it seems
As we learn to see pennies in the sand.

The Mayor, our first White Speaker
Took us back to an ancient plan
Eating with our White brothers and sisters
Where once we couldn't buy the land.

We see you in every embrace
Where men hunger for equality
And no matter what we have to face
We will do it with grace and dignity.

Today, we take another picture
For your likeness may never come again
But history will chronicle this adventure
Where we saw the sunshine in the rain.

Minister Joel Osteen

A man who seems
To breathe God's own breath
And speaks about God
As if he sits down with
The High Master
Every day
Over a cup of coffee
Discussing worldly matters.

Some times I think
That he not only
Has the key to Heaven
But is one of the archangel
In charge of people
On earth and in Heaven.

Just watch him preach
How he caresses the Word
And the intensity
Of the exaltation of the Lord
The skills he possess . . .
The real life stories
The love for family
Friends and enemies.

This man is truly favored
By God and he knows it
And he uses all of his wit . . .
Wisdom and wonder
To convince us to learn
More about The High Master.

Listen to Joel
He is always excited about
What God has made out of him
And what God can do for you.

What a Heavenly spirit
Every Sunday night at twelve P. M.
He pleads for us to come in
And listen to him.

What an exalter
I can hear it in his voice
See the tears in his eyes
And his left hand in his pocket
Like he' going out to gather
The harvest.

He not only preaches
He teaches
Giving examples
Of what God can do.

And he communicates
The Word
So persuasively
So convincingly
So encouragingly
So pivotally
That one is inclined
To listen

Joel
With his "forever" smile
Reminds me
Of the story of David
"A man after God's
Own heart.

As for me
In my long Christian journey
He is the wonder
Of all time
The hope of today
And the curiosity
Of tomorrow.

James Brown

Made Blacks feel proud
When he sang and danced
That he was Black
And he was proud.

I was not only proud
Of him,
But I loved
To hear The Master
Of Soul
Say, "Say It loud,
I am Black
And I am Proud."

He gave us something
To be proud of
Because some of us
Have been made to feel
That if you are Black
There is something
Wrong with you
Something despicable
Sort of like a disease
And no one feels proud
To be in such a situation.

But, The Master Of Soul
Gave us something
To be proud of,
If no more than
To re-examine our thinking
And sing and dance
While thinking about it.

He knew that he didn't
Need to use his color
Or allow anyone else
To put up barriers
To keep him from
Being happy and proud.

Thank you Mr. Brown
For spreading the news around
That you can be Black and proud
At the same time
What women or man
Does not require
A black dress or suit
For that special occasion.

Be proud
Black sisters and brothers
Think of your self as being
Basic and pure as well
As proud
That is if you want to be,
And remember
It is imperative to be proud
And to know, that no color
Can erase you
Un less you agree.

So, like Mr. Brown suggested
Be proud of your Blackness
As well as its richness
And enduring quality.

Mr. Winston Churchill

A man of great thought
Wisdom, and will
Knew when to run
And when to stand still.

He knew when
To grasp an idea
When to seize a thought
And let it become its own
To go where it ought.

He knew to fear was death
So, he put on
The right emotional gear
And talked his way to success.

What he said,
Ate at people's mind
Leading them to resign
Their faulty plan
As he took control
Of the land.

With his mighty rhetoric
And steady grasp,
Of the issue
Made the weaker man
As immobile as a fixture.

Yes, his brave new words
Bought with both,
Laughter and tears
Will always be heard
In history's ears.

Mrs. Gloria Lewis, R. N. Crownsville Hospital Center,
Crownsville, Maryland.
Retirement

I came to Crownsville
When I was young
She was in her infancy stage
I worked from sun to sun
In the very beginning phase.

Crownsville Hospital Center
Became my second family
A place to live and grow
To welcome the coming century.
With its transition and info.

I kept myself informed
Of the good and the bad
With my friends at my right arm
To remind me of what we had.

Oh, the beauty of those years
Documented in time's aging eye
Working with people who had no fears
Encouraged me to try,

To see the opportunities
Of those times
Which I can recall
A chance to work
With some of the best minds
Was there for us all.

I had no degree
To offer the Center
Just my training
Experience, and common sense,

And a feeling of right,
I would not surrender
As my long years give evidence.

I have been on stage
Fourty-two years
With a vision, voice and view
Bold, candid and without fears
Often suggesting,
What the Director
Of Nursing should do.

I am a part,of the past,
Present and future
Of Crownsville, Hospital Center
And I feel I will always be here
As a part of this adventure,

Now, I celebrate
Myself with you
As my very best friends
Grateful to all of you
Who saw me through
To reach this magnificent end.

Mrs. Eleanor Roosevelt

First Lady

Woman of great beauty
Deeper than the skin
More than a president's wife
A great win, and then,

Propelled herself,
By her own power
To realize, when no one else
That she was time's best hour.

Lived a life without fear
Like a tree that gives good fruit
Put on her garment and gear . . .
And walked a royalty route.

Traveled all over the world
More influential than many knew
The flag she loved to hurl
And never worried about the,"Who."

She was everybody's person
Yet, belonging to no one
Discovered what she could offer,
And took the White House on a run.

Member of this organization and that one
Fame claimed her, but she was fates choice
And when the Eastern Star went down
She never realized her loss . . . .

There was no day like, "My Day."
So stated her news paper article
Matchless, as a leader on her way
With the civil rights a special particle.

Daring,never needed a walking cane
Only one heartfelt desire
To give the President every thing
And never ask how or why.

Only one aspect of her being
Which she closed her eyes to
Something others were seeing . . .
But she held a different view,

To see the President through
Always holding out one arm
Realizing he need someone
To come home to.
And someone to brave the storm.

Mrs. Madeleine Albright

First woman to become
Secretary of the United States
Appointed with great might . . .
To match the work
Previously conducted by men.

But she had enough honors
To argue her place
From the best Universities
In the United States.

Born in Prague, Czechoslovakia
And met freedom in America . . .
Educated at some of our
Best learning centers
And spoke several languages
Fluently.

Appointed by President
Bill Clinton
Who was quick to realize
This lady could do the job
As well as men.

Her proven and demonstrated
Ability
Speaks for itself
Her signature pin
Never left her chest
And the rest is history.

Yes, she was bright and bruised
Love, death, separation
Left their mark
But in her remarkable energy

And fine-tuned resiliency
The traumas tended to harden
Her grip, on the goals ahead.

She has a global mind
And a global approach,
Half enough was never
Enough.
But she did say," politics
And religious matters
Can work together
To promote peace."

She had a great influence
On American foreign policy
But was not admired . . .
By the Iraqi press
Who referred to her as,
"An unparalleled serpent."

We leave to history
Our first and last question
Was she as concerned,
Compassionate, candid
And competent
As a man,
Or the men who
Came before her.

Nat King Cole

King of improvisation
A smooth and relaxed singer
With a velvety voice
Whose talent,
Came easy to play the piano
And sing.

His gift of improvisation
Came early
Providing a pathway
For songs as, "Route 66",
And, "Straighten Up
And Fly Right."

The velvety and husky quality,
In his voice, drew many followers
And accolades.

He began playing the organ
At the age of eleven
And at the age twelve
He was singing and playing
The organ, in his father's
Church, under his mother's
Direction.

Early in his career,
With his smooth, relaxed
And romantic style
The women who listened
To him, nicknamed him,
"King."
"And it stuck ever after."

He formed his own band
"The Rogues Of Rhythm."
And bearing it's name,
Stole a lot of rhythm
And seemingly, romantic
Harmony,
Of special love songs
And delivered them
To the world
In such, an unforgettable
Style.

King was the first Black Man
To host a variety show
Then went on to achieve . . .
World-wide fame
With his baritone voice
And that seemly, competitive
Look,
On his face, following
A performance,
"Try That."

He was "king,"
Of such songs as:
Mona Lisa, Smile.
The Christmas Song
And Unforgettable.

His daughter, Natalie,
Still sings the song
"Unforgettable," with him.
Christmas would not . . .
Seem like Christmas
If we could not listen

To the Christmas Song
Sung by him.
The King of "popular songs,"
"Beloved by million."

Paul Simon

An American Singer, Guitarist
Actor, Writer and Producer
The One-Half of The Singing
Duo of Simon and Garfunkal

Simon and Garfunkel
Were friends since high school
It has been noted that
In addition to his strong interest
In music,
He liked base ball
And Afro-Americans.

As a matter of fact,
He has taken on some
Cultural constraints
And made his music.
More beautiful.

He is very savvy
Has a lot of chutzpah
Loved by college groups
"Draws on music of previous
Decades and literary influences."

He has numerous awards
And accolades
He was the first musical artist
To receive, The Gershwin Prize
And a two time inductee
Into the Hall of Fame
For popular Songs.
Time magazine, selected him,

As one of," THE 100 People
Who Shaped The World."

He is a musical Icon
Who has broken down
So many cultural barriers
With his music,
That not only people
Can feel his genius,
But I think it has helped
Him to identify it within
Himself.

President Bush

Some people say you
Stole the presidency
But I don't think so.

From the get go
I watched you
In a frequency of high regard
Which made me think differently.
Fate seized you for its leading star
To be featured in its show of woe
You didn't know . . .
That fortune would turn her back on you,
And schedule you on a long tragic trip
Where you would never have the chance
To greet the people
With waves of happiness.

On this deadly express
You were left there
With the raging Hussien
The Iracq war
The Katrina claim
And the murderous
911 pain.

The echoing planes of 911
Where the people had no chance
To choose heaven
Or to pray for life.

All of this sadness
You had to contend with
With no stops in between
Madness on every scene
And the people . . .
If you said, "Yes."
You were wrong
If you said, No."
They took the spoon
Leaving you hungry
Crying for food for thought
Yet, you walked on
With that empty stomach
Through the raging storm.

One comforting factor
You knew that one day
With God's will . . .
You would go home
To Laura
Where you could sit down
In a place of love
And write to us
"Points Of Decision."

President John F. Kennedy

We have mostly stood still
Since you left us
We have not found a remedy
Do deal with what
Our country ask of us.

We still ask so much
Of our country
But what we can do
For our country
Is fraught
With many ambiguities.

What a travesty!
We killed the ones
That had a vision,
Made statures of them
In our failure
To look within our selves.

Had we asked ourselves
What we could do for
Our country, as you advised
We might have been able
To save your bother, Bobbie
And your friend Martin
To help us find
The answer to your question.

Now we spend most of our time
Washing that old dried blood
Off of our guilty hands
And finding comfort . . .
Sitting in chairs of discord.
Only a few of us
Have learned from the past
Or dare ask
As Chris Matthews does,
I n, "Tell me something,
I don't Know."

President Lynden Baines Johnson

Liked to be called L. B. J.,
Especially when things
Were going his way.

And he had a lot of ways
That determined his progress
From a young man,
He wanted to further himself
And he looked within himself
And found that he could advance
In life if he met and dealt
With people who had made
Something of themselves.

So, he was a man that
Would develop a plan
That could rise from
The lowest level,
To the top
And remain there
As long as he wished.
It to.

He was always prompt
No one ever had to wait
For him
Well organized
Ambitious and passionate
About all his pursuits
And got things done.

When he left the navy
He went in to politics
And what a politician
Held all four of the elected
Offices of the United States:
Representative, Senator,
Vice President and President.

Became president,
Upon the assination,
Of President Kennedy
And with a land-slide
When he ran for
The presidency.

He was confident
In his domestic policies
Boasted by his experience
"Johnson Treatment,"
(His powerful coercion)
Ability.

He advanced legislature
And designed,
"The Great Society,"
And, "The War ON Poverty."

He was very popular
And most people followed
Him.
Inspired many
With his, picture posturing
Smile
And coercive style.

Loved to talk about the
The Civil Rights Plans,
And said, admiringly,
And energetically
"I am carrying through
The plans of John F. Kennedy,
Not because of our sorrow
Or sympathy, but because
They are right."

Had a good presidency
Until the Vietnam war
Dragged on,
Then his popularity
Began to decline
Think what this did . . .
For a man who was
Always prompt
In getting things done.

President Nixion

Speak, Mr. President, speak,
Speak loud and clear . . .
Don't let the people eat
Contaminated meat of bear.

Speak, Mr. President, speak
Don't let water stand at the gate
Don't let disgrace make you weak . . .
Hurry, say something, before too late.

Take the tell-tale tape
That seems to offer proof
Bring the people from the gate
And stop pretending to be so aloof.

Speak, Mr. President, Speak
Don't let the people command
Or take you to impeach,
Taking power from your hand.

Speak, Mr. President, Speak,
Try to get the people to understand
That you have tried to be discreet . . .
You are not a dishonest man.

Speak, Mr. President, speak,
Remove from behind the gun
And keep to your highest feat
Whatever you do, don't run.

You have the power to set the pace
For a seemingly, distrusting nation
And the opportunity to erase
Whatever the allegation.

Speak, Mr. President, speak,
Tell the people that you love them,
Meet the disgruntled in the street
And listen to their smallest whim.

Written in 1975

Quincy Jones

A Renaissance Man
His music has led him
From band leader
To composer, arranger,
Author and television.

It all started in his puberty
Being bored with nothing
Good to do,
He ran into a piano,
Played a few notes
And fell in love
With the sounds
He heard coming
From himself,
And never looked back.

He filled his mornings
His days and nights
With any one or place
That he could make
The sound of music.

From the piano to the trumpet
To small bands
And towns in America
To big towns in Paris.

Yes, he was constant
In his pursuit,
To broadened his artistry
In the music world
And was unstoppable.

Now he is a giant!
Moving quietly
From the times
Of the famed Billy Holiday
To write music for,
The Great Michael Jackson
And his world renown, "Thriller."

The renaissance of his prodigy
Can be noted in the scores
Of,"The Fresh Prince Of Bel Air
And Alice Walker's Color Purple.

Quincy is a boy who became
A man
Who in his childhood reached
For the moon,
Whose passionate grasp
Seem smaller than a spoon.

But a special melody
Interrupted him
With musical notes and tune
That seemed higher
Than the moon,

Now, partially
Assured of success
With ideas of home
He thought without
Further duress
And ate the spoon.

Ray Charles

Was one of the greatest
Musicians and singers
Of all time.

He was born with his music
And his sight,
But he lost his sight
By the age of seven,
But his musical ability . . .
Kept growing strong
Making people
Love him . . . .

His music was loved
World-wide
And the many honors
Are legion.

He was blind
And didn't have
To see the music
Because the music
Saw him,
And always spied
On him from within
Almost with a spiritual
Whim,
And, "Became his mistress."

The biography claims:
He was an orphan at fifteen
But he took his music
And found a place for himself,
In every body's home.

From the downs
To the ups
From the maid and butler
To the Kings and queens
He didn't have to see
The way the ordinary
Man's sees
To be great.

He could feel and smell
The harmony,
Did you ever hear him sing
"Georgia?"
The home of his birthplace.

He was at home playing:
Jazz, blues, gospel, country,
Rock and roll and western
Truly a musical genius.

With all of his musical genius
His greatest gift,
With the exception
Of being favored by God,
Was his mother, who taught him:
There is no blindness
For one who wishes to see.

His last album, entitled.

"Most genius love company"
Possibly, the things that
Makes them great,
Are least understood by others.

There drive is different and more
Inborn
Something takes them places . . .
No one else has ever been
It seems as if they have no
Choice,
They have been chosen . . .
Not so much for themselves
But, for what they can give
To the world.

Ode To Representative Larry Bell

You must have held your head up high
You must have laughed when you wanted to cry
You must have said, I will try
If others can do it, then why can't I.

You must have felt sheer delight
Like the freshness of dew on a morning bright
And said to your self, "Why hesitate?"
Or be afraid of making a mistake.

You must have been seized by a magnificent dream
That empowered you with the means
To review the legacy on display
And identify a part that you could play.

You must have had an unusual vision
Prompting you onward through indecision
You must have seen the light at the end of the tunnel
While men around you continued to fumble . . . .

You must have kept your goals high
While others casually walked by . . .
You must have said the time is, "Now."
While others about you asked, How . . .

You must have worked diligently to make this flight
And saw the dawn of morning on the darkest night
You must have seen your way clear
And told your self, you could make it there.

You must have seen a mackerel sky
While men of lesser strength walked by . . .
You must have delved deep in to your soul
And asked God to shape your role.

Sarah Vaughn

An American Jazz
And popular singer,
Who brought,
"High artistry" to the music world.
She was one of jazz's greatest
Singers for, "almost half a century."

Her voice was quite rich
With a, "distinctive style"
Some critics claim,
"It brought her fame beyond
The confines of jazz,"

She studied the piano
At age seven
And at age twelve
Became organist and soloist
Vocalist at mount Zion
Baptist church in
Newark, New Jersey.

She was discovered
By the Great Billy Eckstine
At the Apollo Theater
On Amateur night
And won the first prize
In her rendition
Of "Body And Soul."

Sarah was referred to as,
"The Divine One"
With one of the finest
Voice ever applied to Jazz.

All the musical giants
Hailed her
And credited her
With a voices near divine
Listen to her sing "Misty"
And "Body and Soul"
And see how you feel . . . .

Steve Jobs

Today October 5, 2011
Steve Jobs died
Co—founder of Apple Computer
And various other
Significant devices relating
To man's communication
With one another.

A genius lived amongst us
Until today
Who transformed the world
Manifesting near Godly talents

In his visionary approach
For the earth,
But not of the earth.

He was born for greatness
His mother's greatest gift
After birth,mandated
That he be exposed
T o atmorpheres
Of higher learning.

Just the exposure
Ignited that genetic might
Into an electrical energy
That burned through
The thoughts of ordinary man
To become ashes of beauty
In fifty-six years.

The Mcintosh, Apple,
Ipod. Iphone Ipad
And only *God* knows
How many thoughts and pieces
Of genius he held quietly
In his creative soul.

We can only mourn and grieve
The loss of this great man
But if we have any understanding
Of what he gave the world
We will rejoice and smile
And know that *God* never
Takes more than He gives . . . .

For we will see those
Penetrating eyes
Every time we use
The computer,
The Ipod, the Iphone
And the Ipad.

Think about him
We didn't lose him today
For he never belonged to us
He was a gift on loan from *God*
Who today returned
To his rightful owner
Leaving with us his gifts.

Tyler Perry

An American Actor
Director, Playwright
Screenwriter, Producer, Author
Songwriter,and Entrepreneur.

"Used God's little flashes of light"
And went from living in a car
To a mansion,
Rags-to-riches
And used his creative energies
To build an Entertainment Empire.

Tyler, do you think
That your meteoric rise to fame
Has anything to do
With your with-holding
Your childhood pain,
And that your character Medea
Has the answer for everything?
Or do you think your father beat
Your creativity out of you
"Who seemed to think that beatings,
Were the answer to everything"
Or had no idea at the time
That this childhood pain
Would plant the seeds for fame.

But, Tyler Perry
Seeing what you went through
I'm not going to worry
About the poor Afro-American man

I know he can make it
If he thinks he can.
You are a living example . . .
Who went from an abused child
To an ambitious and successful man.

From living in your car
To a mansion
From a penny to a million
From Tyler to Medea
And had the inspiration
To take some of us with you.

You have demonstrated
That dreams do come true
And I would like to say . . .
In the American way
You are the epitome
Of the American Dream.

WE-Nursing

We were not put here
To compare our tasks
Our gains or our woes
We were put here
To love and to care,
And embrace
Each opportunity
To serve others.

We are here to utilize
Our concepts
Of a healthy
Body, mind and soul
And exemplify
The being of others.

For in the promotion of others
Reside, hope, love and faith
Strength and courage
And perhaps the only justification
For our extistence.

Thus, we pray
With every single accomplishment
That our work become
More significant to those
We serve,
Than any dream we ever held.

Let each act be intensified
With the joy of being and sharing
Our knowledge and strength
With those who are more deprived.

Written, 1966, while teaching The Sisters of Charity at
The Seton Psychiatric Institute, Baltimore, Maryland.

Whoppie Goldberg

An American Comedienne,
Actress, Singer, Talk show host.
Author, Political Activist
Broadway Star and Producer.

You are the epitome
Of the American Dream
Who possibly,
Laughed and cried
Your way to stardom.

Won all the awards
That ordinary people
Can win,and those
That they can't.

But you are not ordinary
You were born with unique talents
To own your self,
And suffer the consequences.

So, early in life,
You liked your differentness
And never tried to hide it.
As a matter of fact,
You learned to prize it.

Even as a child,
As you walked down that
Lonely road of life,
Putting comedy
In the strife
And walked on by.

Never played the maid
You are among, "The very elite
Group of artist"
Highly acclaimed
On Broadway,
With the creation of your
One Woman show.

Hosted The Academy
Award Show Four times,
Never expecting the show
To come to you
You went to the show.

Used your blackness
To share your beauty
Of thought,
Never letting anyone
Put you in a box.

You made the angry heart
Laugh
In comedy,
Always as crafty as a fox.

Got The mark Twain
Prize for American Humor
In The Color Purple . . .
Your genius was portrayed
In showing the beauty
And love of Blacks
Where everyone could see,

That's where some Blacks
Achieve their trophy.
You create, innovate
And personate

Made your first performance
At a children theater,
At age eight.

In the political activist
Realm
I see some new insights,
You have assumed
That Blacks were owners
Of them selves
Possibly, by the progress
That you have made
And the statement
That you made 11/7/2011
In regard to whom
Blacks belong to
Keep your political acumen
And look behind you
As you host The View.

Thank God for people like you
Who will speak out
When some one should
To clarify a matter
Because no one
Should have to walk
In some one else's shadow.

To President Elect Obama

You are more than a great orator
For you take ordinary rhetoric
And embrace it with an elegance
And a voice of sheer delight.

You break your message down
Into tiny little pieces
So that all ages, races and cultures
May seize a bite,

That is not only appetizing
But chewable to those without teeth
And who have long lost the savor
For the political ambrosia,

Find your words not only palatable
But sweet to their hungry souls
Filling them with a desire
To try and reach the sky.

Hearing your words
We no longer walk
We are tempted to fly
With our broken wings
In these troubled times . . . .

We smile again,
Singing in voices high
Thinking of the change
That you speak of,
Because we find a harmony
Of thought
Obscured from us
In the past.

Stay put Mr. President
Man only die once
He may think it is more
Because he has so many
Mini deaths during his life.

Just remember, in all
Of your goings and comings
God is not dead,
Despite the fact that
The Great philosopherNietzsche
Declared that He was.

The people didn't understand
Him then, nor do they
In these times
Nietzsche meant that the people
Acted like God was dead
And some of them still do.

I just want to say to you
That God still reigns
From on high
And looks low.

He prevails
Over all we know
And that we don't know
Over both lightness
And darkness
For He never closes
His eyes
On that He created,
And is committed to Him.

Stay!
Through the storm
Heavy clouds

And lashing Lightning
God is here . . . .

No man can usurp
God's control
He put you in the position . . .
And only He can take you out
Stay put . . .
Under His secret light.

Let no man steal your joy
Or your Birth certificate . . .
Nor question your destiny
God is the High Master,
And Overseer . . .
Stay . . .
God holds the winning
Hand . . . .

Rosa Park

Removed the cord
From around our neck
In a stance
That surprised the nation.

Said, "No."
When she was expected
To say, "yes."
In a pleasant stubbornness.

She wouldn't move
Kept her seat
Challenged the old law
Willing to swallow . . .
The poison of discontent.

Comforting herself
In subtle anger
Took us on a long walk . . .
To return
To seats in the front
Of the bus.

Madonna

History has never know
A women
Both, as fragile
And strong as you
Seem to portray.

Are you certain that
You are not more
Than one person
Living more than one
Life.

You have always been
A high achiever . . .
And have seemingly,
Taught yourself
To not really need
Anyone.

You are unparalleled
In most entities
You have been there
Done that
And know that.

You seem to have
Taught yourself in puberty
To be independent
And developed the chutzpah
To argue, debate and defy
Any situation that did not
Suit your fancy or philosophy.
Early in life, you seemed
To comprehend
That living was a challenge
And that to die was to,
Lie down and go to sleep.

Your determination
And grasp on life
Is phenomenal
Your accomplishments . . .
Are staggering
As are your fans . . .
And those who emulate
You
As well as those who
Envy and covet you.

You have influenced
The world
Not as much with your
Artistry
As with your ability
To shock the religious
And sexual mores,

By being your self
Willing to go nude
To persuade and convince
Another that he or she
Is walking in the street
Without any clothes on.

You are a bright sprit in any society
Because you have proved
And demonstrated that you
Want to live out your God given
Potentials
And die later . . .

History will record
Your openness and input
Into life,
And the lives of others
By being yourself
And never flinching
When the fires
Began to burn.

Robert Kennedy

Attorney General
During the Kennedy
Presidency,
An extremely forward
And progressive man
Saw the nation as it was
And raised his hand.
To do something
About the things
That he felt held
The nation back.

He didn't have to seek
Equality
He had it
He didn't have to deal
With poverty
He had never been hungry
He was born in plenty
He didn't have to worry
With the horrors of racism
He was a White man
From the upper class system.
Born into the dynasty
Of the Kennedy clan.

Besides, he seemed to have
Everything:
Good looks, health, training
Education, and a deep respect
For the church,
And more importantly
Love of God and his fellowmen.

But all of these gifts
And favors were not enough
To whet his wit and wisdom
Of what he observed
Heard and felt
Because he was a visionary
And was able to see
The nation as it is today.

The Bible Says, the wise man
Will see sorrow before
The foolish man
And he was wise
And full of sorrow.

He felt the pains and trials
Of the Black:
Inhumanity of Jim Crow
Cries for equality
Poverty
Being hungry,
Poor health,with no choice
But to die
Poor education, if any,
Criminal environment
Unfair penalization
And obscured justice
All of these, seemed
To make him feel
Sick on his stomach.

He fought for the underdog
The Immigrant,the Native
American, and any individual
Who sought the American
Dream.

He was passionate and bold
In his determination:
Placing Civil Rights
As the biggest problem,
Eqality,economics,health
Health and education
To follow,
With a heavy emphasis
On crime.

He was America's man
And was a true giver
Answered calls day and night
Especially during the time
Of the freedom riders.

Afro—Americans loved him
His picture was not only
Hung on the walls of their
Homes,
But, I saw them on their windows
When I traveled to Washington,DC

He was a great legislator
And saw voting as the key
To racial justice.
And possibly the pursuit
Of happiness
For many of us.

He was ahead of his time
He saw today
Over forty years ago,
And tries to tell us.

When he inquired
In his speech at Ball University.
What kind of lives America
Wished for her self,
And implied, those with luxury
Had an obligation
To those without.

Before he ran for president,
He had this to say:
"I do not run for president
Merely to oppose any man,
I run because, I am convinced
That this country is on
A perilous course
And because I have strong feelings
About what must be done
And I feel that I am obligated
To do all that I can."

He was so very fruitful
Like a beautiful apple tree
One without apples,
Could never compare . . .
For they would be free
Of all the sticks
He had to bear.

He was assassinated
As he gave himself to us
But as we cried and debated . . .
We were convinced
That he was made of the
Right stuff.

And if he had to die
He would not have begged
To live,
In a world and not try
To use his God given skill.

General Colin Powell

Former Secretary Of The State

A most decorated individual
More than any of my time
And deservedly,
But this is no surprise to me . . . .

When I first looked
At his photo
I was startled, before
I could move on
To learn more.

His eyes, sharp
And discriminating
Indicated a quick
Assessment of their own
Needing no further thought,
For action.

They spoke
So knowingly
Of him
His past,
Present and future.
They seemed to
Reveal all of him
What he would
And would not do
From the essence
Of him.

He said,"Luck comes
To people that are
Well prepared."

But surely, you cannot
Attribute all your honers
To preparation and luck,
I think it is the work
Of a genius,
Favored by God.

For, no one else
Could lead you to
And through such
Honors and triumphs.

Let us look at some
Of your achievements:
Four Star General
Bronze Star
Soldiers Medal
Legion of merit
Purple Heart
10 military
Decorations
And consultant
To six Presidents.

The wit, wisdom
And wonder
Of such a man
Cannot be explained
Under mere mortal's plan.

Micheal Jordon

Moves the ball
Where he wants it to go
Like no other man
Takes the show.

One look
In his eyes
Leads me to know
How the muscles rise
And he has to go
Where they tell him
To go.

To you Michael
In your landscape
Of time
With your breath
And high energy
The ball field is like
Old wine.
As you move on . . .
To the other side
Of glory.

With that passionate grip
Takes the ball to new heights
In what the leaps
Have been to you
Gives the world new sights
To study your view,

And be what you
Were called to be
The best this side
Of eternity.

Pieces Of History

We are small pieces of history
Wrapped up in times design
A mosaic of life's strange mystery
Sitting on the hands of time.

Some of us are born for greatness
No matter how the dice are tossed
With a DNA that points to concreteness
Where we are found, if lost.

Sometimes we choose a person to lead us
Through a mentality of hate, love or derision
Some of us cry, fight, covet and rebuff
But the wise man knows
That God makes the final decision.

Sarah Palin

Governor of Alaska
Has a lawn filled with a river of desire
Where she opts to handle each storm
In the sea.

With her windy words
And long arms . . .
That reach far beyond
Her physical needs
And her obvious charm . . .
With ideas and thoughts
Without a qualm
That they might alarm
Those with lesser ambition.

Who is Sarah Palin
Does any one know
Lives in a clay house
By the sea and snow.

A political figure
Seems inspired
By worldly disarray
And the tangled political yarn
Likes to get out in the storm . . .
And speculate
Thought by some
To add to her charm.

Quit the governorship
Seemingly
Without blinking her eyes
To sail the dark waters
Of a different size.

Points her gun
At the biggest game
Then smiles
As she complains.

Then hesitates
To drink black tea
Never minding the bitter taste
And as drive meets ambition . . .
She sips a cup of deer soup
That she made in her own kitchen.

Gleeful that she shot the deer
Killed by her own hands
Now in a mammoth strength . . .
Speaks of defeating the president!

Who is Sarah Palin
Does anyone understand her plan
Or what brings her joy
Would she use the American People
As a child uses a toy . . . . ?

Bill Gates

A quick and new thought
Could not wait
For what the schools taught.

Had another way
To walk on the top of time . . .
The class room could not say
Or read his mind.

From an early age
He wrestled with
An unknown God
He had no clear stage
Was it mere camouflage?"

With a quick thought
And brazen mind
He could not be taught
He was ahead of his time.

Inquiring in the early dawn
With an idea that had a mind
Of its own
And dreams that had been drawn
From the marrow of his bone . . .

So, he could not wait for college
To finish him with a degree
With this different kind of knowledge
He had to be free,

To fly with the wind
With this new type of birth
To a world that had no end
And no time for mirth.

Joe Louis

A great boxer
A mild mannered man
Born with a bomb
In his right hand.

He never seemed to know
The power of his hands
Called the Brown Bomber
Held the championship
More than any other man.

He was a credit
To the human race
Giving The Afro-American's deficit
A better learning space.

Heavy Weight champion
Of the world
Undefeated,
In twenty-five fights!
Using the gift given to him at birth
To knock his opponent out.

One of the greatest fighters
Of all time
And according to all arbiters
Destiny was kind.

President Clinton

I liked you as president
You seemed to be in our corner
Even when we expressed
A lot of discontent,
Fret, pause and ponder.

Do you know
You have been referred to as,
Our first Black President
But you are White
Yet, I know what they meant
You made a pivotal investment
In the Black Experiment.

In each event
You showed so much delight
With so much chutzpah
To make the wrong —right.

It doesn't matter
If you are White
You helped us get
Through
Some of the darkest
Nights.

Now we can live better
In the light of day
Because you prized us
No matter what
Some people say.

Send In The Seals

Did the grounds rise up in Jalalabal
While the seals took wings
Thinking of an American Sky
That had gone grey and sad
Where death lie in graves of pain.

Send in the seals
No time to spare
Men with feet of steel
That walk on the air.

Send in the seals
Don't question why
See the ashes in the field
While our people cry.

Send in the seals
Bring him to me
Dead or alive . . .
Though not my style
I would rather see
The eyes of his pride.

Send in the seals
No time to reckon
We will not yield
To this blody beckon.

Send in the seals
The President said
Find the Achilles heel
You know what led
To this turning wheel.
"Send in the seals"

How The Situation Room
Stood still
We can not eat another meal . . .
With specks of blood
On every thing
We have come too far to yield
Not even to our pain.

"Send in the seals"
Once spoken
Seemed more than a command
Like a touch of glory
From an immortal hand
So bold, brae and brain
Seized command.

Something like the hands of God
Allowed a taste of vengeance
For the long decade of waiting
To outwit the devil.

Now the living
Of those who died
Laughed and cried
As they danced in the street
Far from the jungle of death . . .
Where the enemy
Was thought to be.

But all the unrest was met
When the seals found him
In near isolation
From his team
Like a cloistered monk,
Who had forgotten
How to pray
Whom to pray to
And what to pray for.

More Than A Building

The George mck. Phillips Building
Marks the very essence of his being
To reap the true joys of his giving
Is more powerful than eyes for seeing.

For among the great men who came,
Draped in the destiny of a plan
He cherished us and suffered the pain . . .
Of being a friend to man.

While others came and went
The love of this man stayed
Questioning why men without consent
Had to walk streets that were not paved.

In a divine destiny,he gave himself
In a monumental struggle and price
Caring for the blind, lane and the deaf
So they might comprehend the magic of life.

So he leaves to us a legacy
That is ours with clarity of mind
To comprehend the efficacy
Of living in his time.

Sidney Poitier

Clothed in honor and majesty
As endowed as the herbs of the fields
In a proud positiveness
Learned to smell the flowers
Before they blossomed
In his elaborate youth.

No copy –cat
Or papier-mache
Knighted with the golden
Sheen of character
And the wise brain of laughter.
Who smelled the sweet
Breath of respect
Before he received it.

Charming,
Hands need no gloves
Or warning . . .
This is a man
Kingly to say,
"To Sir With Love."

This is a man
Who reached high above
The pettiness of man
As if viewing images of God
In a most noble stance.

We no longer have to "Guess
Who Is Coming To Dinner,
You of course,
For there is a place
Reserved for you
At the head of the table
Because you are you.

Nelson Mandella

What a fellow
Defied the spirits of hell
And lived to tell his story
With such a supreme glory.

Lived within cement caves
Fenced in like barbed wire
Ate his fears . . .
Drank his tears
And walked on,
Through sleepless
Nights of hate.

Defying an assortment
Of punishment
And death
Giving victory
To no one.

And when the strong arms
Of fate asked why
He did not take his life
Or cry for the life he had lost
What they didn't realize . . .
That God was carrying the cross
And Mandella was wearing,
The crown.

Oh, the great Mandella
Where can we find a fellow
Who can bear the strong winds
Of the South
And live in prison
Like it is his house.

Maintaining his soul
As a holy man
Living on an inner plan
While friends inquired . . .
And time expired
He lived on
They would not kill him
And he refused to die.

There was no final prize
Or voice
That would suffice
That entangled motif
To choose defeat
Of a spirit that had no match
No parallels
And no hells.

Stevie Wonder

Wonder of the world
Known as a musical
Child prodigy.
An America's singer,
And song writer.

Seems as if you were born
With barrels of songs
Hidden deep Inside of you
Just yearning to be born.

You began to learn the piano
At the age of seven
Mastered drums,
And harmonica
At the age of nine.

Though you are blind
Your heart sees all of us
In the songs that you write
Which we love . . .
And have come to call
Our own.

They are simple
Yet, deeply profound
As they allow for one
To Feel –out the meaning
Of the song
On a personal
And individual basis.

"I just called to say
I love you."
"You are the sunshine
Of my life."
And, "My Cherie Amour."

Stevie you are a Wonder
Your music is heard
And loved all over
The world.

You make your music fly
You give it wings
Of inspiration
So passionate and hardy
In a big banquet of variety
Frequently, making your fans . . .
Want to have a party.

Mr. Wonder
You are favored by God
Only He
Could give you so much
Creativity.

Keep that, free for all smile
With those strong humanitarian
Principles and thoughts
On human rights,
And continue to sing . . .
The world—wide.

We may never know
The wonder of you
But we know we love you.

Abraham Lincoln

Sixteenth President
Of the United States
A prairie lawyer
Partially a self-made man.

From the beginning
Destiny held his hand,
But, fortune could not
Wait for him,
So fate took command.

Confronted with a nation
Cut in half,
Drowning in a caldron of hate.
While slaves
Sought their freedom.

He called for unity,
But was not heard
Then he became . . .
A man of war and peace.

The war came and went
Taking many lives
But peace nevercame . . .

A man of peace
Who set his mind
On uniting
The North and South
Died for more.

Which he addressed
In The Gettysburg address
Freedom
Not only for the living
But the dead as well.

The land was too raw . . .
With fear and hate
For both master and slave.

Even now, approximately
One hundred years later,
Some old masters
Are still looking for
Their slaves,
And some slaves
Are still looking
For their master.
Neither were prepared
To live without each other.

The legacy of your presidency
Will live in history
And the mystery of your time
Can be found in The Gettysburg
Address
For those who can read between
The lines.

Princess Di

I almost cry
When I think
You had to die
To become
A full-fledged princess.

In death you live
More fluently
Because you broke
The barriers
Between love and hate.

Princess Di
One more thing
You took most of the pain
From the wedges
Of the monarchy.

Now your sons
Will continue your work
They will take the plunge
And continue to give the world
In love and memory
That unfinished part of you
That the world will never forget.

Loniel Hampton

An American jazz Vibraphonist
Drummer,
Percussionist, pianist, actor
Band leader and composer.
King of vibes
Who touched shoulders . . .
With Louis Armstrong.

His mother claimed
That as a child
He was drawn
To any percussion type
Of instrument
And with his, "boundless
Energy"
And inborn showmanship
It was difficult
To afford the drums
That his, seemingly
Creativity
Called for.

He Learned to play the drum
In catholic school.
A Dominican nun taught him,
Her name was Sister Petra.

Being excited with the sounds
He could make with the drum
He began to play the xylophone
With the vibrator.
And became the greatest jazz
Vibraphonist.

Loniel was the first notable
Jazz musician to play the
Vibraphone
And was largely responsible
For the establishment of it's use
In jazz.

He played with Benny Goodman
The King of swing
At a time when Blacks
Were not allowed to play music
With Whites,

But with his great talent
On the vibraphone
And drive for rhythm,
Showmanship and excitement
He broke down . . .
Some of the racial barriers.

He established his own band
"And became one of the best
Known orchestra leaders
Of The Big Band Era."

"He was always a people pleaser"
And became world famous
For his most exciting shows
And talent with the sounds
Of the vibraphone
A talent that no other
Musician had learned to match.

Loniel is largely responsible
For introducing the use
Of the vibraphone into jazz
And to the world.

Did you ever listen to him play
"On The Sunny Side of The Street?"
It seemed that he stayed
On the sunny side of the street
With his drive, passion and joy,
Compounded by his great
Showmanship.
Left the audience staggering . . .
With his riveting music.

Rush Limbaugh

Man of many personalities
First with life,
Treating it like dice
Seeking the still waters
That flows down many alleys
To make a cup of coffee
Black . . . .

Brazen and harsh
In his reach
In a rhetoric
Dare not teach.

Both lean and ball
In his likes and dislikes
Reminds me of an old
Russian wolf pack
Who chews on his prey
As they look back
On drops of blood they shed
Trying to escape . . . .

Learned early
To put up walls
Daring his contacts to fall,
At the most vulnerable levels.

Projects his anger
In near slander
Then hides
While waiting
For a response.

Once he spoke of his anger
Toward the president
A billboard statement
Was a response to be sent
Only ten words of content
Little time was to be spent
So to honor the event
The party member wrote
"Waste no time on Rush's inability
To appreciate the President."
This was the quote.

Lou Rawls is an American Soul, Jazz, and Blues Singer

Actor and voice-Actor
Who lent his rich baritone voice
To many cartons.

He was singing in the church
At age seven,
And as a teenager
Began to sing with local groups.

Rawls sang with Sam Cooke
After graduating from high
School
And was known for his smooth
Vocal style.
Frank Sinatra once said,
"Rawls had the classiest singing
And silkiest chops in the singing
Game."

Rawls sang background vocals
On Sam Cooke's,
"Bring It ON Home To Me"
Too with his silky, baritone voice
And versatility,
He could sing jazz, blues and pop
With little effort.

These are two of his very
Popular songs:
"Winds Beneath My Wings,"
And, "You'll Never Find Another Love Like Mine."

Lou was quite charitable
And utilized his talent
And those of other stars
On his Parade Of Star Telethon
To help Afro-American
College students, The UNCf.

Rawls never lost that gospel
Hint in his love songs
Whether jazz, blues or pop
It was there under the surface
And when he sang
It would always come to the top.

Billy Eckstine

An American Singer,Actor
Who also played trumpet and guitar
He was a bandleader of The Swing Area.

Billy was credited with forming the first
Bebop- big band.
And the first romantic Black male
To perform popular music.

Billy began to sing
At seven years of age
And entered many amateur
Talent shows,
Many of which he won.

He had a smooth, baritone voice
And a great singer of ballads
But he subsequently became
As popular in blues jazz and bop

Most people referred to him,
As Mr. B.
He was handsome…
Of mixed parentage
A style leader
And noted sharp dresser.

But most importantly,
Billy demonstrated a great
Deal of pride in himself
And for others,
And seemed to possess
An intergrated soul.

He formed his own band
And, "made it a fountain head
For young musicians,"
Who reshaped jazz.

At times he played trumpet,
Valve trombone and guitar
There was no band that
"Sound like Billy Eckstine's."

He was a visionary
And a model for musicians
Like: Sarah Vaughn, miles Davis,
Charlie Parker,
And the great Quincy Jones.

He was the first Black popular singer
To, sing popular songs in the Black race
Black bands were forced to stick
With novelty or blues vocal numbers
Until the advent of Eckstine.

In the 50s he rivaled Frank Sinatra
And was dubbed, "The Sepia Sinatra"
Although, he liked to be referred to as Mr. B.
Which made him feel most proud.

He was proud of himself
And his accomplishments
And other musicians felt
This presence.

His chutzpah, and pride

Marked his musical talent
And interest in the talent
Of others
Which increased his popularity…
On a worldly basis.

For example:In the 40s
The south dropped
The prevalent request
That the audience be segregated
By race
Because of Mr. B.'s debonair
Behavior.

He was a legend
And served as a model for
Many of the great Blacks
Of his time and of today,
Because he had a mastery
Over self
And refused
To let himself get in his way.

And changed the course
Of history
Reshaped jazz
And left a legacy of strength,
Hope, faith, hope
And good will.

He was well loved by musicians
They claimed, "He was our singer"
Lionel Hampton, recognized him
As one of the greatest singers
Of all time.

Charlie Parker

An Americian Saxophonist
Considered, "A Jazz Great"
Helped to redefine the entire
Direction of jazz music.

Had a very humble life
Left school at age fifteen
An d turned to drugs
At an early age
While with all of his genius…
Was never able to be healed.

But during his short time
His horn was divine
He could play like a bird
That's how he got the name
Charlie Bird Parker

In the early 40s, he joined
Billy Eckxtine's band
Who encouraged young
Mucisians
So, when "The Bird" perfected
His soloing, he began to look
For new forms
And would experiment
On his own time.

It is said that his style:
"Was blistering,
He moved frenetically
And seemingly effortlessly

All over the scales
Creating a bird-like
Trilling sound
This new and profound
Sound,
Earned him his nickname
"Bird"

He transformed old cord,
Formulas into highly
Exciting new ones,
Leaving his band members
And the audience mystified.

His greatest works
Are those he recorded
In the late 40s on his combo,
No one has ever equaled him
Because he could play
The saxophone
Like a bird singing.

Mrs. Laura Bush

First Lady
Like a quaint rose bush
Holds a thorny rod
In her hand
But rather than force
Or push,
She lets the tearless petal
Give command.

Keeps her steady
And peaceful gaze
On the land
Wbere combat is near
Gazing on the rocks
Out there.

Suddenly, there is
Near hurricane action
Though a rose…
Acting like a cactus
But with her quiet compassion
She blooms on mother's day....

Without saying a thing
In her rosy way
Has the faith
To go in her library
And read
On a stormy day.

Magic Johnson

An American Professional
Basket Ball Player
Philanthropist, Entrepreneur
Motivational Speaker
HIV/Aids Presenter
Has won many championships…
Beginning in High School
And College.

Magic is a great ball player
And there is something magic
About his playing.
He is recognized and honored
As the most valuable player
With a very high degree
Of frequency.

But his greatness
Rest not in the game of base ball
Base ball was just a means to the end
He is a hero in this other game-
The game of life.

When his contracted the disease
Of the century.
He portrayed gentility
By announcing to the world
A story he didn't have to tell

But he knew,
That it is not what happened
To you, what matters most
Is the individual's reaction
To it.

You are not only a champion
On the ball field
You are a champion in the game
Of life
You are a player
Not just for the life we were given
But the lives we give to some one else
When we can forget about our self.

You have won many championships
But label this as the best one of all
For you won the heart of the world
When you had the courage to tell
Us don't' go down that path
I went
And the way you confronted reality
This is what I call more than gentility

You'll never know how many people
You influenced, to walk a safer path
And to not have to suffer the aftermath
You knew that many of us
Needed to be protected from ourselves.

Thank you for being our friend
Advising us to not go where you have been
You may not be seen as a champion
For turning yourself in
But it takes more than a champion
To be a man
And reach out and help others
With a broken hand.

Marvin Gaye

An American Singer, Blues, Jazz
Rock& Roll.

Gaye's live seemed to have
Been determined in his early
Childhood days,
It seemed that he never
Were able to communicate
With his father, who was a preacher
On a satisfactory basis.

It has been said, this inability
To relate to his father
Contributed to a "divided soul"
A soul that has no assurance
Of what is good or evil.

This is what I perceive:
Marvin Gaye
Your father felt that
You wouldn't obey
And beat you nearly
Every day,
Never hearing
What you had to say.

You really never knew
As you grew
That you would be
The artist that you are
But the questions lived
Inside of you
And grew too.

But the questions lived
Inside of you
And grew too.

It seems as if you translated
All of your questions
Into your musical songs:
"What's Going On"
"I Heard It Through The Grape Vine"
And that "Sexual Feeling"

You never found the answer
To your father's attitude
Even when you felt enthused
So you sang, I'll Be Doggone
And Aint That Peculiar.

In all of your hits and wonderful
Talent
You father refused to tell you…
That is if he knew
Bu t the world loved you…
Because you changed
Our quiet attitude
About expressing
Our sexual felling
Now we can sing about it
And keep the harmony.

You received numerous awards
After your death
They just keep rolling in
Every time we think about you
Now and then.

Questions for A Nurse

Did you smile at someone today
Were you able to communicate with them
Did you stop to help them on their way
Did you do it happily and with vim?

How many people have you taught to live
How many people have you taught to love
How many people have you taught to give
Through your teaching, that God is love.

Did you teach one woman to love her husband
And to comprehend the sacreness of the holy bond
That the wisdom of life is to understand
When all the material things are gone.

Did you teach one man to love his wife
And that life is more than having bread and water
And how to find the magic spice
Without one-time saying "Mr. you oughter?"

Did you think of the new-born child
Or the mother who shrieked in pain
Did she see a nurse with a great big smile
Who thought that motherhood was
A Miraculous thing?

Have you taught one child to love his parents
And through them achieve a glimpse of himself
That he is not just another deterrent,
But unique and different from everyone else?

What did you say to the dying man
Who exclaimed, "I'll do anything to live."
Did you calmly offer him your hand
And help him to keep the strength to give,

His life and death back to the giver
And to use his last precious moments
To think,
Of his life as a free flowing river
And when fully appreciated
Never runs over the brink?

A Poem for Olivia B. Jones

You

You were always the happy one
Bringing kind words and a sweet
Embrace
In loving others you had fun
Marked by a pathway of grace.

At Crownsville you saw sad times
Coming
And you wanted people to rejoice…
Not cry,
So you threw yourself into the
Running
And became a hostess
Of the finest choice.

Governed by an angelic spirit
You pursued both beauty and love
And in a sharing-giving merit
You talked with the angels above.

To possess a great sensitivity
That lives inside a person's soul
So they can achieve a touch of eternity
Which is more precious than
Silver or gold.

The good is what mattered to you
Under the canopy of a caring heart
Your plan was to see us through

When it came time for us to part.

It was your choice, not ours
To open doors for state employees
Adorned with sweet words and flowers
So we could experience the many joys.

Too, in working with your clients
You made nursing them one big party
Always guiding them to be self-reliant
With a love so big and hearty.

You would suggest the road best taken
In a few precious and countless moments
Where no one would be forsaken
In any of our nursing care units.

You planned a going away party
Where their hopes could be held high
You braved the storms of the sorority
So we could experience the joys of good –bye

No myth, no quarrel, no debate,
Or innuendo
Could capture or quell your grace
You ran against strong winds,
To the eagle's view
With a smile of triumph on your face.

Your gifts to Crownsville Center
Are legendary
A legacy to which we all can attest
There is no one whom we can compare.

With the true splendor of you as our hostess.

You let love become a reality
With highest regard for every one
To achieve this a rare capacity
And rejoice when the job is done.

Prince Rogers Nelson

Prince is the name most of his fans
Like
He is an Amercian Singer, Actor,
Composer, Director, and Writer.
He is one of the most versatile
Musician
And his music styles include:
Rhythm&Blues, Funk, Psychedlia
And Rock 'n' Roll
It has been said the "Versatility
And quality of his work,
Is indicative of a musical genius".

Prince formed a band in high school
And was later influenced
By James Brown,Jimi Hemdrix,
And"Allied with the tradition
Of Marvin Gaye and Sam Cooke.

Prince mixes"Spirituality and sensuality"
Which may seem to reflect a lack
Of realism in both the spiritual
And sensual world.
But the irony of this, is that what
May first seem detracting
May prove to be both invigorating
And enlightening.

He is always fresh and startling
In his music,
With a great gift to, seemingly,
Give it a life of its own.

In other words, his music
Has an agility if its own.

Prince is a very talented musician
I don't think, that the world
Has been privileged
To see and know of his true gifts
In the musical world
There is a feeling that Prince
Has withheld more than
He has been able to share.

But if one catches a glimpse
Of his many hits
They will immediately gleam
That a genius of music, may be
Lying dormant there.

Ray Charles

Was one of the greatest
Musicians and singers
Of all time.

He was born with his music
And his sight,
But he lost his sight
By the age of seven,
But his musical ability…
Kept growing strong
Making people
Love him….

His music was loved
World-wide
And the many honors
Are legion.

He was blind
And didn't have
To see the music
Because the music
Saw him,
And always spied
On him from within
Almost with a spiritual
Whim,
And, "Became his mistress."

The biography claims:
He was an orphan at fifteen
But he took his music
And found a place for himself,
In every body's home.

From the downs
To the ups
From the maid and butler
To the Kings and queens
He didn't have to see
The way the ordinary
Man's sees
To be great.

He could feel and smell
The harmony,
Did you ever hear sing
"Georgia?"
The home of his birthplace.

He was at home playing:
Jazz, blues, gospel, country,
Rock and roll and western
Truly a musical genius.

With all of his musical genius
His greatest gift,
With the exception
Of being favored by God,
Was his mother, who taught him:
There is no blindness
For one who wishes to see.

His last album, entitled.

"Most genius love company"
Possibly, the things that
Makes them great,
Are least understood by others.

There drive is different and more
Inborn
Something takes them places…
No one else has ever been
It seems as if they have no
Choice,
They have been chosen…
Not so much for themselves
But, for what they can give
To the world.

Sammy Davis

Child Stardom, on vaudeville
Stage
Became one of the most
Famous African American
Entertainers.
He could do practically
Every thing
Dance, impersonate, act
And sing.

What happened Sammy
You never seemed to be
Happy
In fact, with all of that
Talent, you seemed rather
Empty.

Did you allow your
Blackness
To detract from you super-
Human performances
For, you were born with more
Than the average talent.

The mouth could sing
The feet could move
In dance
And the rhythm and agility
Was matchless.

One of the world's
Greatest performers
Hit the heights of Broadway…

But joy was not there
You gave it all away…
Leaving no highs
For your self.

You seem to always
Be looking for that
Other part of self
Thinking it was stored
Some where else.

Oh the choices
All a seemingly
Rejection of self
Rejection of the
Afro-American plight,
Conversion to Judaism
Fascinated with satanism

All of these choices
Embraced by none
Possibly,
Because you stood in
Your own way
Never learning
To prize
Yourself.

Muddy Waters

Whose birth name
Is Mckinley Morganfield
More elegant and distinguished
Than the nickname Muddy Waters
But that is the name he liked
To give his music a different sound.

Muddy is an American Musician
Whose musical influence
Is tremendous
Covering a wide variety of music genres:
Blues, rock 'n' roll, folk, jazz and country.

It has been said that anyone
Who has followed the course
Of modern popular music,
Is aware of muddy's vast influence.
On it's development.

Muddy altered the sound
Of the blues
Reshaping it's course
And the blues have never
Been played like Waters
Played it.
And is generally considered the,
Father of Chicago blues.
And he created a Chicago sound
No one could follow.

In 1958, when he toured England,
This was possibly, the first time
They had heard amplified
Modern Urban blues.

The British were inspired by him
Chuck Berry got his first contract
Through him,
Waters music influenced
Eric Clapton
And the great B,B, King
Had this to say:
It will be years before most
People realize,
How greatly waters contributed
To American music.

The beauty and majesty
Of his music is loved
And remembered
If not well understood.

I had never heard your music
Until the year of 2009
When my husband
Was dying
And a friend, saw me crying,

She sent me some of his music
From the state of Texas,
The Might of the rhythm and harmony
Was like a referee,
Pulled me out of the arms of sorrow
And gave me strength to view tomorrow
And other times

And really enjoy your music

Muddy Waters,
How did you get that name
Reminds me of an assortment of pain
So clouded and polluted
To never feel nothing but rain.

But your life was no such pain
For in the blues you reign
With your genius like ideas
Even you couldn't explain,

The different sounds
And searing harmony
That took you on a spree
Sounding so heavenly
We all could see
That muddy water
Couldn't stand still any longer
And reach the epitome
Of his artistry.

You had to run on
To be free
Of all the debris
To achieve a clarity
More clearer than the sea
With such multiplicity
To be where you belong
Within the pages of history.

There is a muddy Water Drive

Named for you
In your home town of Chicago
Receiptient of the Blues Foundation
Award
A US postage stamp
And numerous other honors
Continue to mark your life
As one of the most influential
Musicians In the development
Of American music.

The Community Unity Ball

Is more than a call
To stand up and be counted
It is to recognize the goodness
Of all men,and to cross all barriers
That would prevent us
From doing so.

In that spiritual knowledge
To put our heads together
And hold hands,
To be committed
To the concept
That, "Together we stand
Divided we fall."

This Unity Ball
Signifies more than the easel
Highlighting the picture
Of this holy man
Or the holy feeling,
Pushing its way
Through the picture frame.

It is pregnant with love
Not just for kinship
Or neighbors, or someone
We know,
Love for strangers
Or individuals
From another part
Of the world
Or angels
Whom God has herald,

To bring us the good news
Of how we can love
One another
A little more.

The Unity Ball
Cast in these wintry
Winds of fall,
With the picture of this man
Against the background
Of food and games
Seems like he is raising
His hand,
Not only to the community
But in remembrance
Of his plan,

That in all we do
In and out of the community
We must learn to love
One another
If we expect to have unity.
That love
Lends itself to unity.

In honor of Rev. Glenwood Hemmingway, a young minister,
the founder of The Community Unity Ball, as a yearly event. He left this
inspiration as he passed away in the prime of his spiritual life.

Elvis Presley

Took the nation by surprise
With a rhythm that touched
The skies.

Stirred the hearts
Of both young and old
In a body language
That riveted the soul.

More than poetry or prose
Touching other worlds,
Of select repose.
Where a sexual gymnastic,

Seem to hold
A great tsumani of joy
That continue to unfold
As his fans grew old.

Still through the eyes of his fans
And the fainting shadows of time
The fairyism at Graceland
Keeps him alive, in their mind.

Nursing

Nursing, in my youth you beckoned me
Before I knew what living was about
But there was a burning fire within me
Like the quickness of a girl scout,

To help someone find his or her way
To remember the brightness
Of their childhood
To help a dying person pray...
And teach that life is good.

To engage the mind and body
In healthy thought and action
To learn the art of love
To work, to dream and be taught
About things that put me above
Those who never sought,

To give with all their heart
And be false to no man
To practice the nursing arts
And be a friend to man.

All the years at Crownsville Center
Readied me for Rica Dear
And each door I enter
Her voice, I softly hear.

Speaking of the wonders of nursing
Making me feel I have seen it all
To be endowed with such a blessing
In God's eyes to be called . . . .

How many hands have I held
How many tears have I dried
A thousand stories,I could tell
Of how I have tried.

I have no yardstick to measure
All the things that I have done
But it has been a pleasure
And so very much fun.

Did I have the healing touch
To help someone find his or her self
Did I love them very much
So a part of me could be left,

To fill them with the joys
Of the morning
So they could triumph over the day
To be at peace with God in the evening
As I go on my merry way.

Written for Mrs. Ludie Sims, R. N., Crownsville Hospital Center,
Crownsville, Maryland

Author's Biography

Lattice Boykin Mckoy, is the sixth sibling of ten, three boys and seven girls, born in Rose Hill NC, to the Rev. and Mrs. L.B. Boykin. She received her RN. From the Community Hospital, Wimington, NC, and her Ph.D, in Human Development from the University of Maryland, College Park, Maryland. Lattice has been writing poetry since she was a child.